Excel Ac

You have decided to take your Excel expertise to the next level. Well done!

Let me tell you what you can gain from the book:

The book exposes the world of macro commands, creating magic in the field of data processing so that you can:

- Save time
- Keep deadlines
- Streamline work
- Get the appreciation of colleagues and managers

So what are you going to learn?

- Right after reading the "Macro Recording" chapter, you will save many hours of work by learning how to record an absolute macro and relative macro. (Yes, there are several kinds of macro recordings.)
- In the "Range Selection" chapter, you will learn how to save lots of time, even if you have never recorded one macro in your life.
- Right after "The Importance of the Cursor's Position" you will be able to automate your files, regardless of the cursor's unknown first location!
- You will save even more time by using the Tips and Tricks that are spread all over the book.

I am looking forward to hearing how the book was useful to you, too!

Maayan Poleg

What is a Macro?

Advanced Excel users encounter repetitive tasks while working, including:

- Reports that need to be produced weekly
- Data that needs to be updated monthly
- Tables that need to be formatted daily
- And more...

Some tasks are easy and simple, and some are very complex and involve many considerations. These tasks typically consume a lot of time that could have been spent on other work-related tasks (or if no one notices, for resting...).

An example of such a routine task is a Daily Sales File from which we need to filter out only the records that belong to our region. Then, we have to copy the data to a new file and view the departments' sales by areas throughout the day.

And although it is a simple action, when you have to do it daily, it is time-consuming and boring.

So what if you could make someone else do this work for you?

What if you could click a button and all these steps will be done automatically?

It is possible with Excel!

Using advanced knowledge of Excel, knowledge learned in this book, we can record the steps or operations that we want to perform, and then press a button to repeat them over and over again (and again).

This wizard is called **"the macro recorder"**

It is a built-in tool in Excel which allows the recording of actions performed on a file.

Proper and effective use of this tool can automate the processes of data tables - whether they are of fixed or variable size, whether we want to work on constant locations or according to the cursor's position, or whether the table is complete or missing data.

This is an effective tool, which records all the actions taken in a file: selecting cells and ranges, data entry, formatting and more. The action is recorded only once, and then it can be repeated again and again at the click of a button. This prevents nerve-racking routine action, helping us have more free time and be greatly appreciated for the efficiency that we start to show.

Macro recording has many advantages. You can:

- **Avoid** routine tasks
- **Save** valuable working time
- **Prevent problems** that may result from human errors!

This is one of the most powerful features that exist in Excel for repetitive tasks and is ideal for saving time and for your work life balance.

The greatest advantage of macro recording is that there is no need to write any code at all, even though the final product is written in the VBA programming language. In fact, the whole process that turns the recording into programming code is done behind the scenes, without your involvement.

Using macros, you can:

- Apply formats and styles
- Manipulate numerical and textual data

- Import data from external sources such as CSV files or TXT files
- Create new workbooks
- Create pivot tables
- In fact, you can automatically do every action you had to do manually.

Table of Contents

On a Personal Note

My name is Maayan Poleg. I have been an Excel expert for the past twenty years, during which I met many Excel users. Most of them are "heavy" users, just like you are.

I've noticed that one of the common requirements was **to automate routine processes** to make the ongoing work easier. However, many users were not interested in learning VBA programming, or planning to do so later.

For this advanced group of users - and if you are here you are probably a part of it - I wrote the book *Macro Recording - without Writing Code* that will get you to a higher level to implement your Excel capabilities and will do it in an easy and friendly way.

I believe that after reading this book and practicing along with it, you will be able to do your work considerably more efficiently. I have no doubt that you'll gain organizational recognition due to your new and improved skills. This will happen faster than you expect, because there's nothing more pleasant to hear than "Meet Michael, our Excel wizard."

> **One of the secrets for effective recording is a good knowledge of Excel and the use of various tricks that you will learn in this book**

Wishing you a pleasant learning experience,

Maayan Poleg

Disclaimer

This book was written for Microsoft Excel users who want to expand their Excel knowledge.

Considerable effort has been invested to write this book which is as complete and reliable as possible, although that does not imply any guarantee.

The author is not responsible for any loss or damage which may be caused to any individual or organization due to the information contained in this book.

It is highly recommended to back-up all work data prior to executing any changes.

The Book's Structure

Much thought and many years of experience in training have been invested in writing this book.

The book is written in a step by step approach; and each step will expose you to the challenges which experienced macro recorders encounter on a daily basis as well as to the advanced techniques and considerations involved in recording macros.

At first, you will learn how to record a simple macro;

Then you will learn how to make informed decisions regarding the data range, for example: Do you want the macro to operate on a predetermined range or a variable range?

Later you will learn

- how to select ranges effectively
- how to use the formulas in the recorded macro
- how to decide when to perform the range selection (before/during recording)
- how to create impressive forms, and avoid making mistakes in data collection

Finally you will get helpful tips such as creating a standard table from a report and importing a text file.

Tips and tricks are integrated throughout the book. They alone can vastly improve your command in Excel and the products you can make with it.

I have no doubts that studying this book will make you an Excel Specialist in your organization!

The book is accompanied by practice files put together specifically to address the unique challenges of each chapter.

The commands and screen shots were taken from an Excel 2013 version.

The display differences between this version and earlier versions (Excel 2007 or higher) are insignificant,

However, there may be differences in the recorded code while executing our steps. In such cases I have tried to present different solutions for the different versions.

Practice Files

In order to make learning easier and to allow you to practice, exercise files were added to the book. Since there are many issues that we will be touching upon, the book is accompanied by many exercises. In general, I have tried to reduce the number of files by putting different types of exercises together in different sheets of the file, unless there is a requirement of having a separate file for the exercises.

In every exercise I will mention the name of the file you have to open, if it is a multi-sheet file, the relevant sheet name as well. File names and sheets names will appear in bold.

Download the files from: http://excel-vba.vp4.me/Macro

And to make your orientation easier, here is the first tip:

Excel Tip: How to navigate the desired sheet quickly

To navigate easily and simply in a file that has many sheets, right-click on the navigation buttons:

(In the versions previous to Excel 2013 four arrows are featured, not two, as shown in the example above)

The next window, which contains the names of all sheets in the file, will open:

*Select the desired sheet and press '**OK**'.*

Learning from this book will improve your command in Excel, so you will be able to make the most of Excel. However, there is a perception that macro recording is a preliminary stage for VBA programming. Those who wish to further advance are welcome to learn from the book *Excel VBA – for Non-Programmers: In Everyday Language*, which takes macro recording one step forward and teaches you to write VBA code without any programming background.

Many years of experience have proven that students who started their VBA study with macro recording arrived to VBA class more prepared.

You can find the book at: http://amzn.to/2cvFvpa (case sensitive)

Who am I and What Can You Learn from Me?

My name is Maayan Poleg. I have been breathing, eating and drinking Excel since 1996. I hold an MA degree in Education, and I'm an active instructor of all of Excel's "cutting edge" applications:

- VBA Programming
- Pivot Tables
- Power BI

I'm a counselor for organizations of various sizes, and the author of the books *Excel VBA for Non-Programmers* and *Pivot Tables - Smart Data Analysis*. These books can be found in academic libraries and are recommended as reading material by various faculties.

Excel VBA – For Non-Programmers is on Amazon's best sellers list!

Excel VBA: for Non-Programmers (Programming in Everyday Language) Apr 14, 2014
by Maayan Poleg

Kindle Edition
$7.97
Auto-delivered wirelessly

★★★★½ ▾ 24

#1 Best Seller in Microsoft Visual Basic

Paperback
$13.57 *√Prime*
Get it by **Monday, Aug 31**

Borrow for free from your Kindle device. Join Amazon Prime

Kindle Store: See all 192 items

More Buying Choices
$13.57 used & new (8 offers)

As a daughter of two teachers, I also chose teaching as a profession.

My greatest ability is to turn what seems to be magical into easily understood language, so that even the most difficult topics are learned easily, which you will realize while reading this book.

A Few Terms Before We Start

Developer Tab

The various options related to macro and writing code are located on the '**Developer**' tab. This tab does not appear on the ribbon by default, and has to be configured for it to appear.

Adding the Developer Tab to Microsoft Excel 2010-2016 version

1. Click on the **FILE** tab.
2. Click **Options**
3. Click **Customize Ribbon**
4. Select Developer, as shown in the following image:

5. Click **OK**
6. The Developer tab will appear:

Adding the Developer Tab to Microsoft Excel 2007 version

1. Click on ![icon] to open the menu.
2. Click ⬛ Excel Options
3. Under Popular, select **'Show Developer tab in the Ribbon'**:

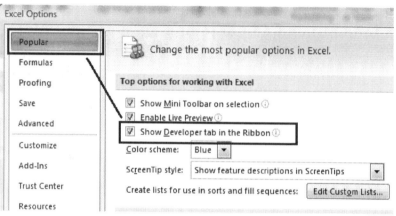

4. Click ⬛ OK
5. The Developer tab will appear:

Security

Security Level

Using macros can optimize processes and improve work efficiency. However, if not used carefully, they can cause lots of damage. For example, a VBA code can delete all the files in a folder.

Therefore, Microsoft has made the macros unavailable by default. However, it does allow the user to change their own security level according to their needs.

> Please note: In order to allow the running of macros, you'll have to downgrade the security level.

Macro Security Settings

1. On the **Developer** tab, in the **Code** group, click ![Macro Security]

2. The following window will open:

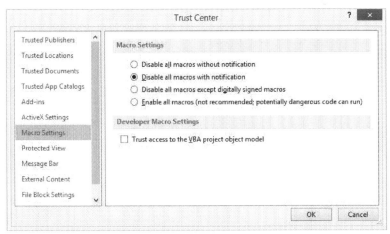

3. Select the desired security level.

Trust Center

Microsoft Office 2007 was the first version to introduce the 'Trust Center', where you can change the security settings of Office files.

Trusted Locations

Trusted Location is a folder that enables the files saved in it to be opened without being checked by the Trust Center's security features.

Make sure to save only files from a reliable origin in this folder.

Trusted Locations Settings
In Excel 2010-2016

1. Click on **FILE** to open the menu.
2. Click **Options**

In Excel 2007

1. Click on to open the menu.
2. Click **Excel Options**

Adding the Trusted Locations

3. Under **Trust Center**, click **Trust Center Settings**, as shown in the following image:

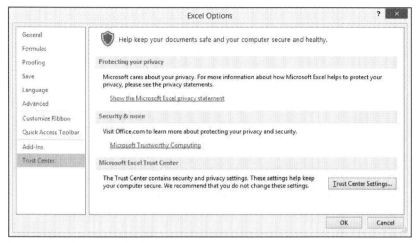

4. The following window will open:

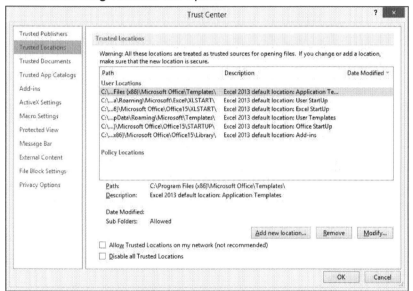

5. Click Add new location.
6. The following window will open:

7. Click Browse to select the desired folder, and then click

   OK .

   You can set the subfolder in the location to also be considered as 'trusted'.

8. The folder will be added to the trusted locations list.

Files with macro commands in the folder will be activated without notification.

Removing a Trusted Location

In the Trusted Locations window, as shown in point 4 above, select the location you wish to remove from the trusted locations list and click Remove

Saving Files

Until the Microsoft Excel 2003 version, files were saved with an "xls" extension.

In the "Ribbon" versions, the extension of the Excel workbook was changed to "xlsx".

And xlsx files **cannot** store Macro commands.

In order to enable the workbook to save the macros, it should be saved with the "xlsm" extension.

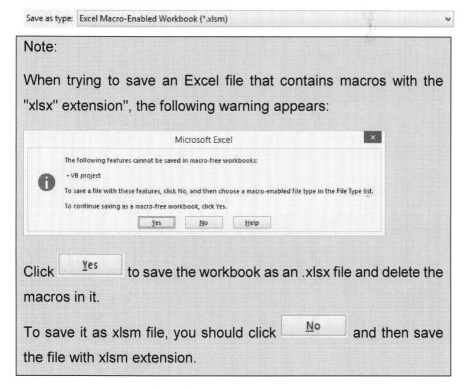

Save as type: Excel Macro-Enabled Workbook (*.xlsm)

Note:

When trying to save an Excel file that contains macros with the "xlsx" extension", the following warning appears:

Microsoft Excel

The following features cannot be saved in macro-free workbooks:

• VB project

To save a file with these features, click No, and then choose a macro-enabled file type in the File Type list.

To continue saving as a macro-free workbook, click Yes.

Yes   No   Help

Click Yes to save the workbook as an .xlsx file and delete the macros in it.

To save it as xlsm file, you should click No and then save the file with xlsm extension.

Important to Know:

Saving the file with the .xls extension will allow you to run macros in the Ribbon versions as well, but it will limit the number of rows and columns in the workbook in accordance with their number in Excel 2003.

(In the Excel 2003 version the number of rows is 65,536, whereas in the ribbon versions the number of rows is 1,048,576).

When saving a file with macros, all the macros are saved inside the file.

If you save a macro in the Personal Workbook (See page 33), when closing Excel you will get the following warning:

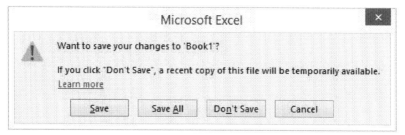

Press "**Save**" to save the macros you have recorded.

A moment Before We Start

Correctly planning the macro actions we need to perform is an important and essential step for achieving the final and desired results. Plan your recording accurately, according to the various considerations that you will be exposed to in this book.

Generally, it is recommended to first perform a 'dry run', i.e. performing all required actions without the actual recording. This will allow you to figure out whether you have considered all the required steps or if you have skipped some of them.

Post the recording, verify that the macro is performing all the actions it had been required to do, and remember to check the following edge cases:

- Does the macro run on a bigger or smaller range than the one you have selected before recording it?
- What happens if you place the cursor in another location (another cell or range)?
- What happens if there is no data at all in the range you select?
- What happens if the cursor is located inside the data range or outside it?
- What happens if the cursor is located near the data range or in a distant location?

I recommend backing up the files, so even if you make a mistake you can always restore the data.

But let's not put the cart before the horse and move on to the next chapter, in which we will learn how to record a basic macro in Excel.

Quiet please... Recording...

Basic Macro Recording - for Automation of Time-Consuming Processes

The basic way to automate processes is by recording a macro directly from the Microsoft Excel software.

Display 'Record Macro' Window

Click on 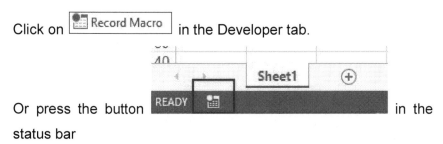 in the Developer tab.

Or press the button  in the status bar

The following window will open:

In this window you will be asked to name the macro (it is recommended to change the default name provided by the program into a significant name that describes the code operation).

Rules for the Macro Names:

- The macro name must begin with a letter (not a number or other sign).

- Spaces are not allowed in a macro name (in other words, the macro should have a one-word name).

- You may use the underscore as a separator between two words, i.e. Sum_Range.

- Do not choose Microsoft Excel's reserved names like "print" or "save". To avoid problems that might arise due to reserved names, you can add the prefix "My", i.e. My_Print to each macro.

- It is recommended to assign a name that accurately describes the meaning of the macro.

- It is customary to combine capitals and non-capitals letters for clarity of reading, i.e SumRange

Note:

An error message will appear if you give a macro a non-valid name.

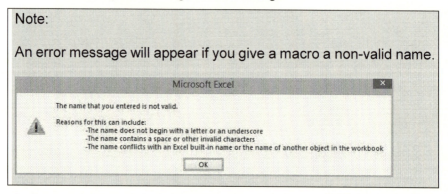

In the next step you will have to choose where to store (save) the macro:

Personal Macro Workbook – the macro will be recorded automatically into the "**Personal.xlsb**" file, which is loaded when Excel starts, and is available for all workbooks.

This Workbook – the macro will be recorded in the current workbook, and will only be available when this file is open.

New Workbook – the macro will be recorded in the new workbook.

You can choose a shortcut key to run the macro.

Please note, there are many shortcut keys in Microsoft Excel software. For example, Ctrl+S is used for saving, Ctrl+P is used for printing, etc.

While assigning a shortcut, the combination you choose will replace the shortcut key action in the workbook where the code was saved. Therefore, it's preferable to use shortcuts that are used infrequently.

You can also add the **Shift** key by holding it down and simultaneously pressing the desired key (there is no need to press the **Ctrl** key, which appears by default).

In this window you can add a description that can remind you in the future what the code is supposed to do.

To confirm, click  .

The macro will start recording your actions now and the button 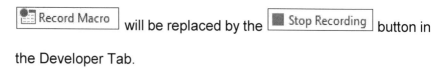 will be replaced by the Stop Recording button in the Developer Tab.

From this moment, everything we do such as selecting cells or ranges, entering data and even formatting (but not selecting items from the menus), will be recorded.

Stop Recording

Click the button  in the **Developer** tab or the button ◻ in the Status Bar.

If you don't stop recording, every action that you perform will be recorded, including running the macro...

Exercise: Recording the First Macro

Our first macro automates a simple yet common action – Formatting (follow the instructions **precisely**):

1. Open the file **exercise.xlsm**

2. Select Worksheet **Format**

3. Select cell A1

4. Click '**Record macro**' 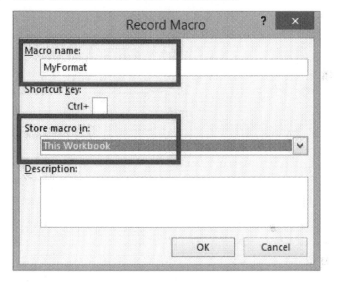 Record Macro

5. Name the macro as **MyFormat**

6. Save the macro in '**This Workbook**'

7. Press 'OK'

8. Using the '**Font**' group on the '**Home**' tab, format the cell as follows:

   a) Bold

   b) Italic

   c) Underline

   d) Blue background

   e) White font color

   f) Font size 20

   g) On the '**Home**' tab, in '**Cells**' group, click on the arrow below Format Option to expand the drop down and

select **Auto Fit Column Width**

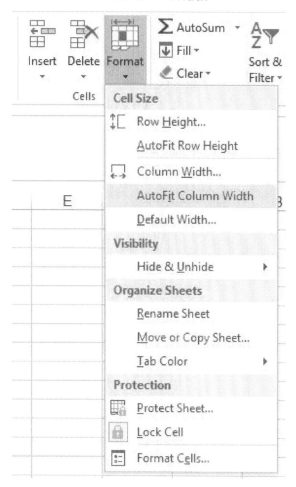

(Use this option to adjust column width and avoid double clicking the line between the columns)

9. Stop the recording by clicking [■ Stop Recording]

Congratulations! You have just recorded your first macro!

How do you run it?

Find out in the next chapter!

Running a Macro - the Moment of Truth...

There are several ways to run the macro you have just recorded.

Note:

> If you are unable to run the macro due to a security level issue, follow the instructions on page 23

Running a Macro from the Developer Tab

1. On the Developer tab, click [Macros]
2. A list with all recorded macros will appear.

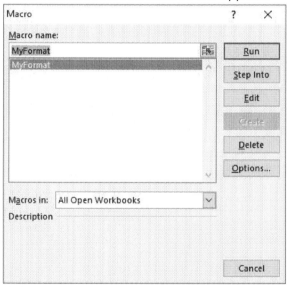

3. Select the macro (you will recognize it by the name you assigned to it during the recording).
4. Click Run.

Running a Macro using a Shortcut Key

1. Select any cell in the worksheet.
2. Press on the pre-determined key combination.

Running a Macro by Assigning a Button from the Form Controls

1. On the Developer tab, click
2. Select a button:

3. Click somewhere in the worksheet.
4. The **Assign Macros** dialog box will appear.
5. Select the desired macro.
6. Click OK .
7. Click the button to run the macro.

Editing the Button

To edit the button, make sure it is framed (if you click on it while it is unframed, the macro associated with it will start running. To select it, if it is not framed, right-click on it).

A right-click will display the associated menu where you can edit the text, assign a different macro, etc.

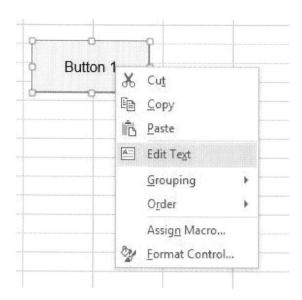

Running the Macro with a Worksheet Object

You can add various objects such as pictures, shapes and even charts, and assign them a macro

1. Select the object
2. Right Click → **'Assign Macro'**
3. From the window, select the desired macro
4. Press **OK**

Running a macro by adding a button to the Quick Access toolbar

1. Click the drop-down arrow in the quick access toolbar and select More Commands:

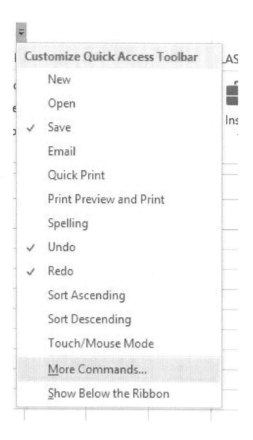

2. In the **Choose commands from list**, select Macros:

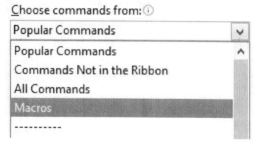

3. Select the desired macro.
4. Click Add.
5. Click [OK].

6. The button will appear on the quick access toolbar:

Customizing the Ribbon (only for the 2010-2016 versions)

Excel 2010/2013 allows you to create new tabs and add macro commands into custom groups in existing tabs.

Creating a new tab

1. Click the **FILE** tab.
2. Click **Options**.
3. From the categories list, select **Customize Ribbon**
4. Click **New Tab**.

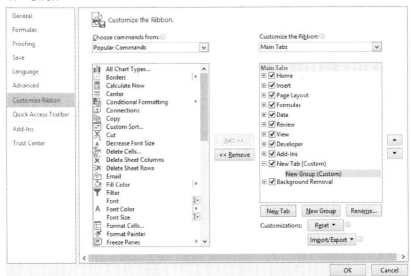

5. The new tab will be added to the ribbon tabs:

6. You can rename the tab by clicking **Rename...** .

Adding a New Group (in a new tab or in an existing tab)

1. Click the **FILE** tab.
2. Click **Options** .
3. From the categories list, select **Customize Ribbon** .
4. Select the tab that you want to add a group to.
5. Click **New Group** .
6. A new group will be created in the tab you have selected:

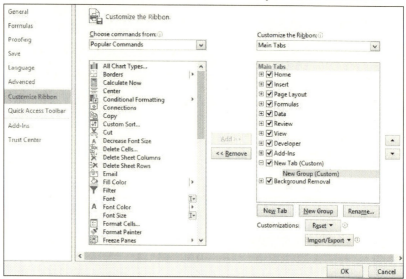

7. You can rename the group by clicking **Rename...** .

Adding a macro to the group:

1. Click **FILE** .
2. Click **Options** .
3. From the categories list select **Customize Ribbon** .

4. Select Macros.

5. Select the desired macro from the list.

6. Select the group that you want to add the macro to and click Add >> .

7. The button will be added to the group you have selected.

8. Place the cursor in cell A1 and run the macro.

9. Place the cursor in cell C5 and run the macro.

10. Select the range F5:K11 and run the macro.

After we've created the macro **MyFormat** as described in the previous chapter, all that's left to do is to run it.

What is the result?

Every cell in the selected range was formatted according to the settings, regardless the range selection; whether we ran the macro on the specific cell it was recorded on, different single cell, or on a range which included more than a single cell.

Deleting Macros

1. On the **Developer** tab, click Macros .

2. Select the macro (you will recognize it by the name you assigned to it during the recording).

3. Press Delete.

Absolute Reference and Relative Reference – Recording Top Secret!

At this point we've learned how to record and run a macro. In this chapter we will learn **the most substantial trick for an improved recording!** But beforehand, let's perform the next exercise:

Record a macro which moves the cursor one cell directly below its current position. For this objective, we will record the next sequence of actions (follow the instructions precisely):

Exercise: Recording using Absolute Reference

4. Open a new Workbook.
5. Select cell A1
6. Create a macro and save it in **'This Workbook'** (the macro will be recorded in the current file).
7. Name the macro as **GoDown.**
8. Press **Enter.**
9. **Stop** recording.
10. Select cell A1 again.
11. Run the macro using one of the methods described in the previous chapter.

If you have performed the recording correctly, cell A2 is now selected. Now, let's select cell B1 and run the macro. Did the cursor go down to cell B2? No! It moved back to cell A1!

What has actually happened?
In order to understand, we have to remember that Excel does exactly what it is asked to do, not what we think we are asking it to do.

In our case, although we had assumed that we had been asking Excel to move the cursor down one cell by pressing Enter, what Excel "understood" was '**select cell A2**'. When running the macro at starting point A1, it only looked like we were moving the cursor down one cell, while actually cell A2 had been selected. When running the macro after locating the cursor in cell B1, we could see our mistake.

Therefore, what should we do in order to really select the cell below the cursor's location?

For this objective we have to understand the difference between absolute reference and relative reference.

Absolute reference – When a macro runs on the specific range of cells that had been selected before recording it, regardless of the cursor's current position. For example, if the cursor is located in cell C9 when we record the macro and we press Enter on the keyboard, the cursor will move to cell C10, and that command will be recorded – 'Select cell C10'. Every time we will run this macro, it will activate cell C10, regardless the cursor's current location.

Relative reference – When a macro runs on a range of cells relative to the cursor's current position. So if the cursor is in cell C9 and we press Enter, the command that will be recorded is 'move one cell down from your current position'. If we locate the cursor now in cell G13 and run the macro, cell G14, which is directly below the cursor's current position, will be activated.

Note that sometimes it is impossible to perform a relative reference operation. If we record a macro that moves the cursor

46

one cell up, and we place the cursor in cell D2, running the macro will select cell D1. But if we run the macro at this location, since the cursor cannot move further up, we will get an error message:

Microsoft Visual Basic

Run-time error '1004':

Application-defined or object-defined error

| Continue | End | Debug | Help |

Click [End] to close the window.

If we click [Debug] it will start the VBA editor for editing the macro.

To close the macro editor, we have to stop it first by clicking **Reset** in the toolbar:

And then close the editor window by clicking [×].

And to continue our discussion, since we recorded a macro using absolute reference, Excel 'understood' that it has to activate cell A2. But if we used relative reference, Excel would have 'understood' that it has to move the cursor one cell down below the active cell, regardless of its location.

How do you switch between relative and absolute recording?

By clicking [🔲 Use Relative References].

When the button has no background color, recording will use absolute reference.

When the button has background color, recording will use relative reference.

Excel Tip: Exiting Edit Mode

Most of us are used to end editing cell content by pressing Enter on our keyboard.

This performs two actions:

- Exiting Edit mode (the state of inserting or editing the content of a cell)
- Selecting the cell directly below the current cell

However, Excel enables us to exit Edit mode and stay in the current cell:

By clicking ✓ in the formula bar

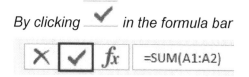

Or alternatively, the shortcut key Ctrl+Enter

Exercise: Recording using Relative Reference

1. Open a new Workbook.
2. Record a macro and name it **MyMacro.**
3. Verify that **'Use Relative References'** is activated (it has background color).
4. Press **Enter** on your keyboard.

5. Type the value 999.

6. End by pressing the shortcut key **Ctrl+Enter** to stay in the same cell where you inserted the value.

7. Stop recording.

8. Delete the content and return to the starting point cell.

9. Run the macro.

10. Select another cell in the Worksheet.

11. Run the macro.

12. Did the macro run relatively, i.e. inserted 999 in the cell directly below **each cell** that you had selected in the Worksheet?

- Important:
- Before you start recording, check whether Absolute Reference or Relative Reference is activated.
- During recording you can switch between Absolute and Relative recording. You can start with Absolute Reference, record a few actions, and then switch to Relative Reference. Later, switch again to Absolute recording and so on as needed. You will find examples further in the book.

Effective Range Selection (Worth Knowing, not only for Macros)

Many actions in Excel manipulate data ranges. Sometimes we work with fixed size ranges and sometimes with variable-size ranges. The following shortcut keys are applied to select ranges of variable or unknown size.

A common example is a table that is imported monthly from an external source that has a different number of records each month but always has to be formatted in the same manner, i.e. adding borders, highlighting headers, etc.

Excel Tip: Useful Shortcut Keys for Worksheet Navigation and Selection

Ctrl+Home *Navigates to the beginning of the worksheet*

Ctrl+arrows *Navigates to the last cell before an empty cell in the arrow's direction. If there are no empty cells in the data, it will navigate to the last cell in the row or column*

Ctrl+Shift+arrows *Extends the selection of cells to the last non-empty cell in the arrow's direction*

Ctrl+* *Selects the region surrounding the active cell, regardless of the region size*

Ctrl+End *Last cell of the used range*

Ctrl+Shift+End *Extends the selection of cells to the last non-empty cell on the worksheet*

Home *Navigates to the beginning (column A) of a row*

Ctrl+Space *Selects an entire column*

Shift+Space *Selects an entire row*

Shift+Home *Extends the selection of cells to column A in the same row as the selection*

> *Whether Absolute reference or Relative reference is used when recording a macro, these shortcuts will always operate relatively.*

Excel Tip: Shortcut Keys that Keep the Range Size Fixed When Recording

The following shortcut keys are used for cell selection and navigating on the worksheet. Recording a macro using these shortcuts will keep the ranges fixed as we selected them. So if for example we select A1:A10, even when the table extends, this exact range will be selected when running the macro.

Ctrl+a *Selects the current region around the active cell. It is different from Ctrl+* which selects a dynamic table, changing the selection dynamically when the table size changes. This shortcut is static, so even if the table size changes, only the range that was selected when recording will be selected when the macro is running.*

Ctrl+.*(dot) Navigates clockwise through the corners of the selected range.*

Exercise: Recording a Macro for Range Selection

1. Open the Workbook **'Select Range'**.
2. Select cell A1.
3. Record a new macro named **MyRange** in 'This Workbook' and perform the following actions using shortcut keys:
    a. Select the entire table range and add borders.
    b. Select the headers row. (Remember to navigate to cell A1 using **Ctrl+Home**. You can also select cell A1 with

your mouse, as long as you verify that Absolute Reference is used.)

    c.   Make the headers bold and change the background color of the cells to light grey.

    d.   Select cell A1. (If you use the mouse, verify that Absolute Reference is used. If you use **Ctrl+Home**, the reference type selected is not relevant.)

4. **Stop** recording.

5. Run the macro on the table in Sheet2 and check if it worked.

6. Run the macro on the table in Sheet3 and check if it worked.

Did the macro work when the table had a larger number of rows (sheet2), and didn't work with a larger number of columns (sheet3)? If so, let me guess: You selected the header line by dragging instead of using the shortcut keys. Remember this: When you select 4 cells by dragging, the macro records a 4 cell selection. However, if you use the shortcut keys to select the header, any columns that will be added to the table in the future will be part of the range that the macro will run on.

The Importance of the Cursor's Position

In the previous chapter we learned how to record a macro to select a range. Before we move on, please open the Workbook '**Select Range**' in sheet4 and run the macro **MyRange.** (The cursor in the Workbook is located in cell H12, so if another cell is accidently selected, please place the cursor in H12 before running the macro.) Did the macro work?

Was a border added to the table?

If you followed the instructions precisely, I assume that the border was added to H12, instead of to the entire data range, as we wanted.

Why did it happen?

Remember: Excel does exactly what it is told to, not what we think we told it to do.

The first macro instruction was "select the region surrounding the active cell and add a border", but since the cursor was located in a cell with no data surrounding it (H12), the border was added only to the active cell.

This exercise's objective is to demonstrate the importance of the initial cursor position: As long as the cursor is located in any cell inside the data range, and we record the range selection by using Ctrl+*, the entire table is selected, even if it changes in size.

However, we cannot ask the user to run the macro when the cursor is located inside the data table, and he may run it when the cursor's position is outside the table. And as we have already experienced, the result in this case is adding a border to this one cell where the cursor is located, instead of adding it to the entire table as expected.

Therefore, the cursor's initial position is crucial: We have to move the cursor to the starting position as part of the recording! Actually, the first action should be selecting the starting position, instead of selecting the table.

In our case, since the macro should run on the data table which begins in A1, the first action that we have to record is pressing the shortcut keys Ctrl+Home to move the cursor to the starting position. (We can also select cell A1 using Absolute Reference.) Only then can we select the entire table. This is how we will make sure that the actions will always be performed on the desired range, instead of running on a random cursor location.

Does the Macro Run on a Currently Selected Range, or on a Predetermined Fixed Range?

Sometimes we want to record a macro that runs on a fixed range, for example a macro that will change the width of column A or format a table in the range A1:D10. In other times we want to record a macro that runs on a range that has been previously selected in the worksheet, for example changing the selected column's width (any column, as long it is selected) or formatting the range that has been previously selected in the sheet (any range, as long as it is selected). Therefore, we need to decide either to place the cursor in the desired range before starting the recording or to record the range selection/cell location as part of the macro.

If we select the column before the recording and record the required actions only afterwards, the macro will work according to the 'selection'. This means if we select a certain column, for example column B, and we run the macro, it will run on column B, and if we select another column, for example D, it will run on column D.

On the other hand, if we record the column selection in the macro, one of the two following situations could occur:

a. Using Absolute Reference, the column that we select will always be selected, so if we record selecting column B, the macro will always run on column B.

b. Using Relative Reference, the column that will be selected is the column that is located relatively to the cursor. So if the cursor was placed in column B and we record the selection in column A (one column to the left), and then run the macro located in column F, column E would be selected.

The following examples will clarify this issue:

Recording a Macro to Change the Selected Column's Width

1. Open a new workbook.
2. Select any column in the worksheet, for example – column D.
3. Record a macro named **ColumnWidth.**
4. Change the column width to 20 by right click the column name → '**Column Width...**'
5. Stop recording.

6. Select another column and run the macro that you have just recorded.

Explanation: Since we didn't record the column selection in the macro, Excel got the instruction "change the current column". This is why when running the macro it runs on any column that is selected in the worksheet.

Recording a Macro to Change a Certain Column's Width – Absolute Reference

1. Verify that Absolute Reference is activated (i.e. the button '**Use Relative Reference**' has no background color).
2. Record a macro named **FixCol.**
3. Select column B.
4. Change the width of column B to 30.
5. Stop recording.
6. Select **sheet2** and run the macro.

Explanation: Since we recorded the macro using Absolute Reference, and we selected column B, every time we run the macro, the actions are performed on column B.

Recording a Macro to Change a Column Width - Relative Reference

1. Place the cursor in cell D1 in Sheet1.
2. Verify that Relative Reference is activated (i.e. the button '**Use Relative Reference**' has background color).
3. Record a macro named **RelCol.**
4. Change the width of column C to 15.
5. Stop recording.
6. Place the cursor in cell G1 and run the macro.

7. Place the cursor in cell J3 and run the macro.

Explanation: Since we recorded the macro using Relative Reference, when the cursor was located in any cell in column D, and we've changed the width of column C, i.e. one column to the left, every time we run the macro, the column to the left of the cursor is modified. (Be careful to avoid running the macro when the cursor is in column A, because this is the leftmost column.)

Recording a Macro to Change the Background Color of a Cell

1. Record a macro named **ColorA1** that will change the background color of **cell A1** to red.
2. Stop recording.
3. Record a macro named **ColorActive** that will change the background color of the **selected cell** to red.
4. Stop recording.
5. Clear the worksheet formatting.
6. Check the macro actions that you recorded on various cells in the worksheet.

Handling Empty Cells in a Data Range

In this chapter, as in the previous one, we will continue discussing the problems that we may **experience,** in order to learn how we can **avoid** them.

For this purpose, follow the following instructions:

Exercise: Finding the Last Cell

1. Open the file "Service calls".
2. Select the Worksheet "**calls**".
3. Create a macro in this Workbook named **AddNewCall** and record the following steps:
   a. Press **Ctrl+Home** to reach the top of the table (starting point location).
   b. Press the key combination **Ctrl+Down key** to move to the last non-empty cell in the column.
   c. Verify that the button '**Use Relative References**' is active and select the cell below the activated cell by pressing the Enter key.
   d. Stop recording.
4. Enter new call details.
5. Run the macro.
6. **Examine** – Did the cursor move to the new empty line after running the macro?
7. Switch to Worksheet '**calls – partial**'.
8. Run the macro.
9. Did it work? Is the cursor now placed on the first empty cell below the data range?

The objective of this exercise is demonstrating the importance of the question, "**Are all the cells in the data range filled with data, or there are any empty cells in the range as well?**"

We have recorded a macro assuming that all the cells in our range are filled with data, therefore we were expecting that pressing the key combination **Ctrl+Down key** would move the cursor to the last non-empty cell.

However, in the Worksheet '**calls – partial**' there is one empty cell located in column A, cell A5. Therefore pressing **Ctrl+Down key** moved the cursor to the cell right above it, cell A4, instead of navigating the cursor to the last cell in the column.

So what should we do if there is a possibility of empty cells in our data?

For this purpose, we should think counter intuitively!

Instead of moving from A1 downwards, we will move up from any cell outside the data range.

We will record using absolute reference in a cell located outside the data range, i.e. if we know that we have 100 records at most, we will move to cell A200. Now we will be able to use **Ctrl+Up key** to reach the last value in the column.

This method works only if the data range never spreads further than the location of the cell that we selected.

Excel Tip: How to Navigate Quickly to a Cell Outside the Range

In order to navigate quickly to cell A200, you can scroll down the screen and place the cursor in the required cell.

A faster way to do it is typing the cell address in the name box and pressing enter.

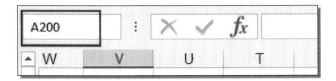

Note, when using this method the reference type - relative or absolute - has no importance; the cursor will always move to cell A200.

Recommendation: Do not try to solve the problem by using Ctrl+End, since there are cases in which you won't get the 'real' data end, but any cell outside the range that may have had value earlier. This option, although it seems reasonable and comfortable, may be found as problematic.

This is one of the cases when using excel VBA provides a solution to each one of the edge cases with a simple short code.

Another Solution: Replacing Empty Cells

As the key combination Ctrl+arrow navigates the cursor to the last location before an empty cell, we can replace all empty cells with space to only make them look empty while they are actually filled with a value (a cell containing a space is considered as a cell filled with data).

We will open the 'find and replace' window:

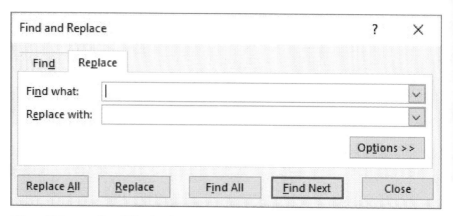

We will leave the '**Find what**' box empty.

In '**Replace with**' we will type one space (by pressing the Space Bar on your keyboard).

Now our data range contains no empty cells.

Using Functions and Formulas

To this point we have learned how to record a macro that navigates within the worksheet, enables selecting cells absolutely or relatively, and formatting the ranges we work with. However, the main strength of Excel is performing calculations; therefore this chapter will be dedicated to the use of formulas and functions while recording macros. We will start with a single formula, continue with summing up unknown range size, and finally learn how to drag formulas across variable-size ranges.

But just before we proceed, since most of the users are not aware of the difference between formulas and functions, let's make things clearer. Formulas and functions have similar roles: performing calculations on the data and returning a value.

The **formula** is written by us, using mathematical operators, for example:

=A1+A2+A3+A4

Function on the other hand, is a built-in formula in Excel. For example:

=SUM(A1:A4)

It is possible (and sometimes even essential) to combine formulas and functions. For example, adding tax (in our case, 5%) to the sum of the cells:

=SUM(A1:A4)*1.05

Exercise: Formulas

1. Open the file **Exercise** in sheet **Arithmetic Progression**

	A	B	C	D
1	1			
2	2			
3				
4				
5				
6				
7				
8				
9				
10				

2. Record a macro named **Calc:**

   a)   Use the shortcut **Ctrl+Home** to place the cursor in cell A1 (even if it is already there).

   b)   Use the shortcut **Ctrl+Down key** to move the cursor to the last non-empty cell.

   c)   Verify that '**Use Relative Reference**' is active.

   d)   Press **Enter** to move the cursor one cell down, below the active cell.

   e)   Write a formula to calculate the sum of the two preceding numbers. In our case, the first action will enter 3 in cell A3 which is the result of the formula =A1+A2

   f)   To finish entering the formula use the shortcut **Ctrl+Enter.**

   g)   **Stop** recording.

   h)   Run the macro several times, and check the sequence.

   i)   Switch to worksheet **fill** and run the macro. Was the value added in the right place?

As you have probably noticed, the macro added the formula to cell A3 instead of adding it to the last cell. This happened since our range contained empty cells, and the action **Ctrl+Down key** placed the cursor right before the first empty cell, which in our case was inside our range, not at its edge.

Sometimes this is exactly the action that we want to perform, so what should we do if we want to reach the last cell even if there are empty cells in the range?

Remember: Think **counter intuitively**!

All you have to do in this case is go bottom up: record a macro that selects any distant cell in column A, for example A1000, using the shortcut Ctrl+Up key to move up to the last cell, and using Relative Reference move down one cell.

Dragging Formulas and Functions

In the last exercise we've added a single formula to the worksheet. When we wanted to continue calculating, we ran the macro again. However, in most cases, when we use data tables, we have to write a formula and drag it across the table.

Let's examine this case:

Every once in a while we get the following table:

	A	B	C	D
1	First Name	Last Name	Date of Birth	
2	Ruth	Weiss	11/08/1985	
3	Jenny	Johnson	09/23/1990	
4	Nicole	Prichard	06/13/1997	
5	Dave	graham	05/01/1999	
6	Michael	Levin	05/01/1999	
7				

And we may have to concatenate the first name and the last name into one cell and erase the original data cells. Additionally, we may have to add another column which contains the name of the month, derived from the birth date.

Before we learn how to record this macro, let's learn a few Excel tips:

Excel Tip: Concatenating Two Text Cells

To concatenate two text cells into one, we will use the following formula:

=A2&" "&B2

The formula takes the value in cell A2, concatenating (adding) it with a space character and then concatenating the value in cell B2.

=CONCATENATE(A2," ",B2)

In both cases, the result is "Ruth Weiss"

Excel Tip: Four Ways to Drag Data Effectively

First way – By using the fill handle (the bold square on the lower right side of the cell), we will drag the formula to as many cells as we need:

	A	B	C	D
1	Product	Price	Quantity	Total
2	Computer	150	3	450
3	Keyboard	20	5	
4	Mouse	5	7	
5	Printer	400	2	
6				

Second way – Double clicking the fill handle will drag the formula automatically until it gets to an empty cell.

Third way – *Using the option 'Fill:*

1. *Enter any required value in the first cell.*
2. *Select the desired range.*
3. *Select on* **'Home' tab** → **'Fill'** → **'Down'**

Fourth way – *By copying.*

This is a sophisticated way that enables us to drag the formula, even if we don't know along how many cells.

Observe the following table, which displays the product prices and calculates the tax:

	A	B	C
1	Product	Price	Tax Inclusive
2	Computer	150	=B2*1.05
3	Keyboard	20	
4	Mouse	5	
5	Printer	400	

We would like to drag the formula across the entire product table.

1. In cell C2 enter *the formula* and end by entering **Ctrl+Enter.**
2. **Copy** *C2.*
3. Using Absolute Reference ('**Use Relative Reference**' has no background) move to cell A1.
4. Move *down* by using the shortcut **Ctrl+Down key.** In this way we verify that we've reached the end of the data table.

If your data tables could have empty cells, instead of moving down from A1 move up from a distant cell in column A outside the data range, as we have already learned.

And why not select cell B1? Because column A will most likely always be filled with data, and column B might have empty cells that

haven't been entered a value. It is 'safer' to use column A than using
column B.

5. *Switch to Relative Reference.*
6. *Move two cells to the right, so the last cell where we are supposed to enter data will be selected. In our case, this is cell C4.*
7. *Press on the shortcut **Ctrl+Shift+Up key** to select all the cells that are supposed to have formulas (in our example the range C2:C4).*
8. *Press **paste.***
9. *The formula was pasted now in all cells.*

Press Esc to remove the dashed border shown around the range of cells after copying.

Each one of these methods is effective in different situations:

Dragging the desired number of cells will set the recorded range size, therefore if the range changes, dragging will be done on the same range that had been selected in the recording.

Double click is convenient and simple, but it also sets the range. Moreover, if there is an empty cell in the range it may stop there instead of reaching the end of the data.

It seems that the Fill option overcomes these issues, but if the first row contains a header and the second row contains a formula, the header will be dragged across the range instead of dragging the formula as we want.

Using the fourth method, copying the data, should work in most cases, as long as the column that we use as a helper column to find and identify empty cells will always be non-empty.

70

The next tip combined with '**Fill**' will help us overcome the problems that we have mentioned earlier.

Excel Tip: Selecting a Range from the Active Cell to any Required Cell

1. *Place the cursor at the upper edge of the range. If there is a header row and underneath that a formula row, place the cursor in the cell that contains the formula, not in the cell that contains the header.*

2. *In the name box, type the address of the other edge of the required range:*

   (If you don't know which is the last cell, select any distant cell that you are sure is empty.)

3. *While the cursor is still in the name box, press the shortcut* ***Shift+Enter***

4. *The range between the starting point (where the cursor is now) and the cell address that was entered will be selected.*

5. *Now the option '**Fill**' can be used to apply the formula across all the range.*

6. *What should we do if the formula has been applied on a range that is too big? The Tip '**deleting rows from the end of data till the end of the worksheet**' on page 75 will solve this problem.*

Excel Tip: Using a Dynamic Table

Over time, our data tables change in size. If we use a formula on a table (the function VLOOKUP, for example, is a function that works on an entire table) but the table size changes, we have to find a way to tell Excel what is the right range now. When we define our table as dynamic, Excel understands that this is the same table, even if its size changes!

The easiest way to do so is placing the cursor inside the table and

selecting  on the '**Insert**' tab.

The next window will appear:

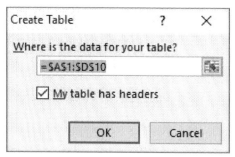

We will verify that the right range has been selected and press '**OK**'.

(Another way to get this window is by pressing  in '**Home**' tab or with the shortcuts Ctrl+T or Ctrl+L). This turns the data table into a dynamic table. When we place the cursor inside the data table the tab '**Tables tools**' appears, including various options relevant for dynamic tables.

We can notice that the name given to the table by default is '**Table1**':

Table Name:

Table1

I advise you to change the table name to a more significant one (for example , Data) by selecting the allocated system name and typing the desired one instead.

Now, if we add data to the original table, we can see that the range of the dynamic table that we have created has expanded, and the new data is included in it!

The use of dynamic data has big advantages. In a pivot table built on the basis of a dynamic table, for example, it is unneccesary to change the data source after changing the table size, just to refresh it.

Another advantage is that writing a formula in one of the cells will automatically drag it across the entire table, so there are cases when using a table is the appropriate solution.

Important to know:

When pressing the shortcut Ctrl+Up arrow we will reach the first empty cell at the edge of the data table. However, when using a dynamic table and pressing this shortcut, we will get to the last cell in the data table; whether it is empty or non-empty. The following illustration will clarify this issue:

	A	B	C	D
1	Product ▾	Price ▾	QTY ▾	
2	Computer	150	3	
3	Keyboard	20	5	
4	Mouse	5	2	
5	Printer	400	7	
6	Computer	150	4	
7	Keyboard	20		
8	Mouse	5		
9	Printer	400		
10	Computer	150		
11	Keyboard	20		
12	Mouse	5		
13	Printer	400	↑	
14				
15				
16				
17				
18				
19				

If we place the cursor in any distant cell in column C, the shortcut Ctrl+Up key will bring the cursor to cell C13, which is the last cell of the dynamic table.

If we worked with a regular table, the shortcut would have placed the cursor in cell C7, which is the last non-empty cell in column C.

To solve these issues that arise when we look for the last non-empty cell instead of the last cell in the table, we can record a macro that converts the table to a range via '**Table Tools**' tab → '**Convert to Range**':

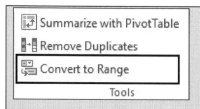

And right after finding the right cell, create a dynamic table again.

Excel Tip: Retrieving the Month Name

When we have cells that contain standard dates (i.e. dates that the character separating between the day, month and year is a slash, for example 12/31/2015), we can retrieve the month value by using the function Month:

=MONTH(A1)

Excel Tip: Deleting Rows from the End of the Data to the End of the Worksheet

But first, if the rows are empty why is it necessary to delete them at all?

One of the reasons is that sometimes we get data from external sources, and although the amount of data is small, the file size is big. This usually happens because Excel usually handles cells that appear empty like those which contain data or some design information.

If we delete these cells, the file size will substantially decrease.

Another possibility is if we dragged a formula across a range which was bigger than the data range, we can reach the first empty cell in the column that contains real data and delete all the rows from this location on. Using this method we can erase the excess data in the formula's column.

1. *Locate the cursor in the first non-empty cell at the edge of the data.*

2. *Press the shortcut **Ctrl+Shift+Down key.***

3. *Press right click and select '**Delete**'.*

4. *The following message will appear:*

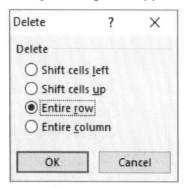

5. *Select '**Entire Row**'.*

6. *Press '**OK**'.*

All the rows that have been previously selected will be deleted

Excel tip: Changing Column Width

*The standard way to change the column width is by right click on the column name → '**Column Width…**' and typing the desired value.*

It is also possible to change the column's width by placing the cursor on the boundary between the column names (for example – between A and B), until it becomes a two direction arrow. Then drag the column left or right to the desired width.

Moreover, it is possible to automatically expand the column's width, to fit exactly the text, by double-clicking the boundary between the two columns. BTW, if you select the entire worksheet and double-

click the boundary between any two columns, all the worksheet cell widths will adjust to fit the text.

Exercise: Fixing a Table

In this exercise we will use two methods to fill in data.

This is a long exercise with many steps, Excel tricks, and switching back and forth between Absolute and Relative Reference. At this point, follow the instructions precisely. Later in the book we will learn how it is possible to split complicated tasks to separate simple macro instructions, and later merge them to run the merged code.

1. Open *the* file **Functions And Formulas** in **workers** sheet.
2. Record a macro to format the table according to the following instructions:
3. Verify that Absolute Reference is used.
4. Insert a new column between B and C.
5. Type in cell C1 the header **Full Name.**
6. In cell C2, write a formula to concatenate the first name and the last name (using the character **&** or the function CONCATENATE – see page 68)
7. After you complete the formula, press the shortcut **Ctrl+Enter** to stay in the same cell.
8. Copy the formula.
9. Select cell B2 (remember that you are using Absolute Reference).
10. Press the shortcut **Ctrl+Down key** to reach the end of the data.
11. Switch to Relative Reference.

12. Select one cell to the right (i.e. the adjacent cell in column C, which is the last cell that should contain a formula).
13. Press the shortcut **Ctrl+Shift+Up key** - the entire range that is supposed to contain the formula will be selected.
14. Paste the formula.
15. Switch to Absolute Reference.
16. Select column C (Since it is a specific column, you have to verify that Absolute Reference is used).
17. Copy.
18. Paste as values. (Don't know how? Read the tip on page 111)
19. In cell E1, type the header **month.**
20. In cell E2, use the MONTH function to retrieve the month value from the date.
21. Press the shortcut **Ctrl+Enter** to exit editing mode.
22. Select all cells from E2 to any distant cell in column E (for example - E1000).
23. On '**home**' tab, select **'Fill' from the Editing group** → **'Down'**.
24. Select column E.
25. Copy.
26. Paste as values.
27. Using the name box, select cell A1000.
28. Press on the shortcut **Ctrl+Up key**.
29. Switch to Relative Reference.
30. Go down one cell. (Now you're in the 'real' end of the data.)
31. Press the shortcut **Ctrl+Shift+Down key** to select all the empty cells in the column.

32. Right click with your mouse.

33. Select 'Delete'.

34. Select 'Entire Row' and press 'OK'.

35. Switch to Absolute Reference.

36. Delete the first name and last name columns.

37. Adjust the column size to display all the data.

38. Select cell A1.

39. Stop recording.

40. Run the macro on the data in worksheet Emp.

Writing Functions to Handle Variable Data Range

We often need to add a summary row to our data tables.The problem with that is that our tables vary in size, and it seems that recording a macro with a function does not give a solution to a computation on a range that changes its size.

One of the solutions is to use a cell outside the table, for example – B1, and to sum the entire column, for example:

=SUM(A:A)

We have to verify, of course, that there isn't any further data beyond the table to avoid adding it to the sum. However, I am about to tell you how to write a function that can handle a data range, even if its size changes!

But in order to do so, let's first learn the next tip:

Excel Tip: Absolute Reference

As experienced Excel users, you probably know that dragging in Excel is relative. So if a function refers to cell B2 and we drag it downwards, the reference will change to B3, and later to B4 and so

*on, as you can see in the next example when we calculate the tax
for each product in the list:*

	A	B	C
1	Product	Price	Tax Inclusive
2	Computer	150	=B2*1.04
3	Keyboard	20	=B3*1.04
4	Mouse	5	=B4*1.04
5			

*In the example above we used a constant value to represent the
tax, but it will be more appropriate to use a helper cell, which is one
cell, in which we will enter the tax value and to which we will refer
each time we want to calculate the total value including tax.*

*In this way, if the tax changes, we will update it only in one cell,
instead of updating all the cells containing tax with the new value.
Take a look at the following example:*

	A	B	C	D	E
1	Product	Price	Tax Inclusive		Tax
2	Computer	150	=B2*E2		1.04
3	Keyboard	20			
4	Mouse	5			
5					

*Every time that the tax value changes, we will change it in the helper
cell (E2), and the total including tax will be updated automatically.
Now, let's drag the formula, so all the prices will be multiplied by the
tax value:*

Let's take a look in the formulas:

	A	B	C	D	E
1	Product	Price	Tax Inclusive		Tax
2	Computer	150	=B2*E2		1.04
3	Keyboard	20	=B3*E3		
4	Mouse	5	=B4*E4		
5					

This is exactly where the problem is!

While we do want the reference to the prices in column B to be adjusted, i.e. that we will refer to B2, B3 and so on, we do not realize that the tax value in the helper cell E2 will change when we drag.

So how do we do that? **Using absolute reference!**

Absolute reference means that we keep the original helper cell absolute although we drag the formula.

In the formula that is in cell C2, we will point to cell E2 and press F4 on the keyboard.

To our surprise we got these results:

	A	B	C	D	E
1	Product	Price	Tax Inclusive		Tax
2	Computer	150	156		1.04
3	Keyboard	20	0		
4	Mouse	5	0		
5					

What actually happened here?

Dollar ($) signs will be added to the cell address.

=B2*$E$2

Now we will drag the formula, and see that the reference to the price column changes while the tax value reference is the same.

	A	B	C	D	E
1	Product	Price	Tax Inclusive		Tax
2	Computer	150	=B2*$E$2		1.04
3	Keyboard	20	=B3*$E$2		
4	Mouse	5	=B4*$E$2		
5					

And here are the results:

	A	B	C	D	E
1	Product	Price	Tax Inclusive		Tax
2	Computer	150	156		1.04
3	Keyboard	20	20.8		
4	Mouse	5	5.2		
5					

And before we move on, it is important to state that you can convert entire ranges to absolute, not only single cells.

So now let's return to the issue of using formula and function in macro recording.

I've promised to tell you the secret so there it is:

The secret is to use absolute reference only to the first cell of the range. So if we are asked to sum up the range A2:A10, we will write the following formula:

=SUM($A$2:A10)

If we use absolute reference only to the first cell of the range while writing the formula, if we run the macro on a variable range, the macro will always know to use the right range!

Exercise: Summing the Data in a Table

1. Open the file **Functions And Formulas** and worksheet **Totals** in it.
2. Record a macro to calculate the totals (product of Price and Qty).
3. Stop recording.
4. Select worksheet **Totals 2.**
5. Run the macro.

Working with Files

Since the macro's main target is rerunning the same set of operations over and over again, there might be situations when we will want to run it on different files. Therefore, this chapter discusses the various perspectives of file management.

We will learn:

- How to run the same macro on different files that have a similar structure
- How to combine few periodic files into one central file, which we can later manipulate according to our work needs

Running a Macro on Different Files that have the Same Structure

We often receive files, and need to manipulate them in a similar way. For example – an external system sends us a report that contains the monthly calls. We only have to filter the technical call records, then perform all sorts of calculations and format the data. Although these are different files, since their structure is similar, we can record one macro, save (store) it in the '**Personal Macro Workbook**' to make it available for all files. Each time we receive a file, we will run the macro to process it.

Since a macro which is saved in '**Personal Macro Workbook**' is available for all files, verify that you run it on the right file.

Here are few nice tips that will serve us as we proceed:

Excel Tip: Quick Filtering

*If we select the cell that contains the value which we want to filter, and we right-click, a related menu will appear. We will select **'Filter'** → **'Filter by Selected Cell's Value'**:*

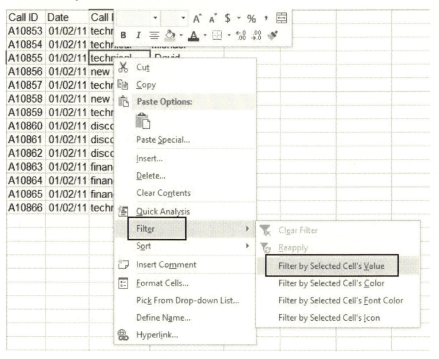

Only records that contain the value which is in the selected cell will be displayed.

This is a smart, quick way to filter desired values.

Recording a Macro to Process File Data

Each month we receive a file containing sales data of various products. We are interested in displaying only the printers and then count their numbers.

Instead of repeating the same actions each time, we will record a macro to help us speed up the process:

Exercise: Processing a File

1. Open the file **Sales – Jan.**

2. Record a macro in '**Personal Macro Workbook**' with the name **FilterAndCount.** (In this way the macro will run on any file.)

3. Place the cursor at the beginning of the worksheet using the shortcut **Ctrl+Home.**

4. On '**Home**' tab → '**Find and Select**' → **Find** type the desired value. In our case 'printer'.

5. Press '**Find Next**'.

6. Press '**Close**'.

7. Press right click → '**Filter**' → '**Filter by Selected Cell's Value**'.

8. Now you have to copy the technical calls data to a new worksheet. Use the shortcut **Ctrl+*** to select the entire table.

9. Press '**Copy**'.

10. Add a new Workbook.

11. Press '**Paste**'.

12. Press the shortcut **Ctrl+Down key** to reach the end of the data in column A.

13. Using Relative Reference, go down one cell and move one cell to the right so the cursor will be located at the end of column B.

14. Type '**Total**'.

15. Move one cell to the right so the cursor will be located below the last data cell in column C.

16. Use the function SUM to sum the sales values, as we learned in page 82. (Make sure that the beginning cell address of the range is absolute.)

    =SUM($C$2:C37)
17. **Stop** Recording.
18. Open the file **Sales – Feb** and run the macro.
19. Open the file **Sales – March** and run the macro.

Recording a Macro for Collecting Data from Files with Different Names

When we record a macro that refers to other files, the file name is recorded as well. This means that when we run the macro, it will search for a file with the same name and path. There are many software programs that produce files with a constant file name and save it to a certain location. In this case, there is no prevention to record the file name in the macro.

But what happens if the files are saved with different names, for example, 'January Data', 'February Data' and so on?

In this case, if we record the file name in the macro we will come across a problem when we run it on other files with different names.

Here are two ways to solve this issue:

a. Using a hyperlink.

b. Saving the macro in '**Personal Macro Workbook**' and running it from the periodic files instead of the main file. Or as we have already learned '**think counter intuitively**'.

Excel Tip: Hyperlink

A Hyperlink is a clickable link that enables us to navigate to other cells, files or even webpages.

The way to add a hyperlink is as follows:

1. Place the cursor in the cell where you want to insert the hyperlink.

2. On '**Insert**' tab select [ ], or press **Ctrl+K**

3. The following window will appear:

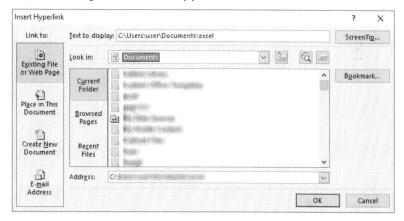

4. Navigate to the desired file using the window '**Look In**'.

5. Select the desired file name from the list in the window center.

6. Press '**OK**'.

7. The cell will turn into a hyperlink, and pressing it will open the desired file.

Exercise: Recording a Macro to Run on Different File Names

Preparations

In any cell in the worksheet, insert a hyperlink to the first file which the macro will run on.

Macro recording

1. Record the macro - the first action is pressing the hyperlink, in this way the macro will open the file and manipulate it as needed.

2. Stop Recording.

3. When you want to run the macro on another file, manually

update the hyperlink first by pressing .

But the Ultimate Solution – Think Counter Intuitively!

We have a file where we need to accumulate periodic data. As we have learned before, we can record the macro in the accumulating file (which is the main file) that will open each periodic file (using either a file name or a hyperlink), copy the data to the appropriate location, and manipulate it as needed.

But I recommend you think counter intuitively. Instead of recording the macro in the main file and each time opening another periodic file, record the macro in any periodic file, and open the main file from within the macro.

Since the main file is only a single file, it has single name and single location, it is no problem to refer to it while recording or running the macro.

We will of course save this macro in '**Personal Macro Workbook**' so it will be available for all our workbooks, and that's it. There is no need to worry about different names of files or workbooks!

Exercise: Collecting Data

1. Open the file **Sales – Jan.**
2. Record a new macro named AddData. Make sure you save it in '**Personal Macro Workbook**'.
3. Using Absolute Reference select cell A2.
4. Press the shortcut **Ctrl+Shift+Right** to select the entire first data record.
5. Press the shortcut **Ctrl+Shift+Down key** to select all the records.
6. Copy the data.
7. Open the file **Annual Data.**
8. Move to a distant cell in column A (A10000, for example).
9. Press the shortcut **Ctrl+Up key.**
10. Using Relative Reference, move one cell down.
11. Paste the data.
12. Save the file.
13. Close the file.
14. Stop recording.
15. Open the file **Sales – Feb.**
16. Run the macro.
17. Check whether the data has been added to the file **Annual Data.**
18. Open the file **Sales – March.**
19. Run the macro.
20. Check whether the data has been added to the file **Annual Data.**

Automation using Forms

One of Excel's best options is creating a form which enables the user to enter information. After entering the data in the form, all that is left for the user to do is to press a button and the data will automatically be transferred to a data collection table!

Before we learn how to do this, here are few useful tips that can help to perform this task.

Excel Tip: Transpose

In Excel there's a built in option of converting vertical data to horizontal or vice versa:

1. Select the desired data range.

2. Copy the range that has been selected.

3. Place the cursor where you want to paste the data.

4. Right click and select:

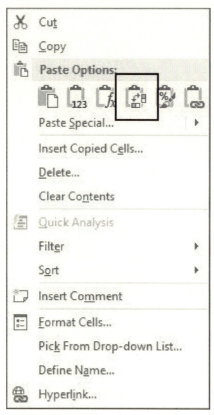

Comment: In older versions – select '**Paste Special**' and in the window that will appear check '**Transpose**':

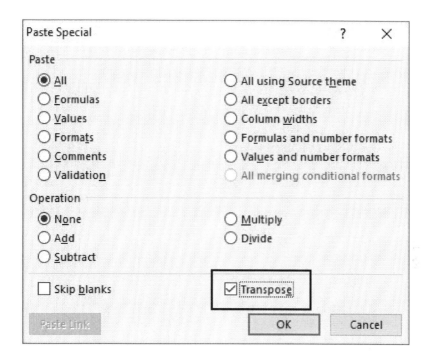

Exercise: Entering Data in a Form

1. Open the file Entering form data.

2. Create a macro which copies the worker names that were entered in the worksheet **data entry** to the worksheet **Accumulated data.**

3. The data is supposed to be accumulated, i.e. each macro run will add the new data to the existing data in the accumulative table.

Dividing Up the Task:

Below are general guidelines for performing the task:

1. First, we have to fill in the fields with data. (Food for thought: Does the data have to be filled before or after the recording?)

2. Afterwards, we have to copy the data.

3. Then switch to the other Worksheet.

4. Navigate the empty cell at the end of the data. (Remember to use the shortcut keys and Relative Reference).

5. Paste the vertical data horizontally to the table, using 'Transpose'.

6. Return to first worksheet and press **Esc** to exit selection.

7. Clear the data and prepare the form for the next record insertion.

8. Place the cursor in cell B1 to prepare the next record insertion.

9. Stop recording.

Entering Data to a Form - Handling Errors

The assumption in the previous exercise was that whoever fills in the form fills all the required data. This assumption of course is proven wrong in practice, when data might not be filled in some fields either accidentally or because the user just doesn't have it; while the critical data is the name in column A.

Why does column A contain the critical data? Because if the name is missing when transferring data to the sheet "**accumulated data**" the following situation will occur when pasting:

	A	B	C	D
1	**Name**	**Address**	**Department**	
2	Dan	NY	management	
3	Rachel	Jersey	HR	
4	David	Jersey	procurement	
5		NY	management	
6				
7				
8				
9				
10				

Currently, everything is OK, but next time we paste the data, and since we're approaching upwards from below the table, the cell that will be selected is A5, and pasting the new data will run over the existing data ('NY', 'management').

The next example demonstrates the problem that might occur:

1. Open the file **Designed Form.**
2. Enter the data in all fields (student name, class, exam date, grade).
3. Record a macro to collect the data from all fields and paste it to the worksheet **Accumulated data.** (That's right, since currently not all fields are filled with data, you have to copy the info from each field and paste it in the right location.) Don't forget when you finish recording to clear the form's data and prepare it for the next record insertion.
4. Stop Recording.
5. Now, enter only the class name.

6. Run the macro that you've previously recorded.

7. Enter data in the form again, this time making sure that all the details are there, and run the macro.

8. Check the data **Accumulated data** worksheet. What happened to the data that has been entered in the previous section?

As we have already realized in the previous exercise, the problem occurs because part of the data was missing. Since our method is approaching the empty row upwards from below the table, if we find an empty cell, we will run over the existing data or even spread the data across two lines and ruin the database.

So how do we solve the problem? Read the following tip:

Excel Tip: Using Helper Cells

Although our table's data is vertical, we can use helper cells and by using a simple formula copy it vertically.

We will start with the simple formula:

I would like to copy the student name to cell A7, therefore I type in A7 the formula =B3.

To B7 I would like to copy the exam date, so I type there the formula =B5.

Continue in the same manner with the rest of the data as you can see in the following example:

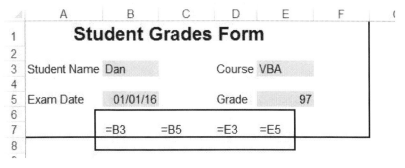

And this is the result:

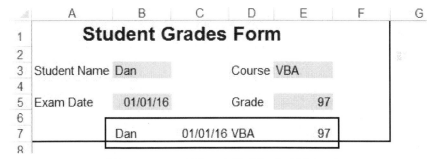

In this way we will be able to copy the data at once by selecting the new range, which includes the formulas, although the data is spread across different locations in the form!

And before we proceed to a more complicated formula, let's take a look at the following example:

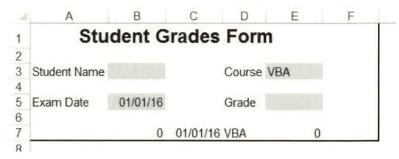

I haven't entered the student name in the form so the digit 0 appears instead of it. While it may not cause a problem when it appears in student name, and even mark the need to enter manually the data in the accumulative worksheet, 0 in the grade, as seen above, would mean failing the class.

In this case, we will use the IF function that will help us make the substantive decision of which value to enter instead of the missing one.

I personally prefer entering space because it looks empty, while it is actually a "gap filler" and Excel refers it as a non-empty cell.

So this is the fixed formula:

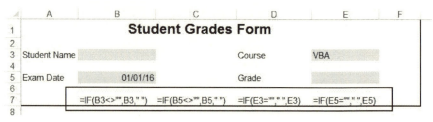

Notice that I've used two different versions of IF for practice purposes. In the two on the right, I checked whether the cell is equal to an empty cell. On the two on the left, I've checked whether the relevant cell is not equal to an empty cell.

This is the result:

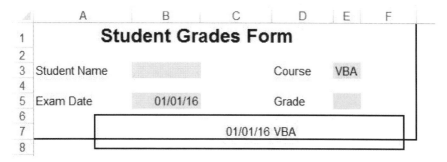

Important: Cells A7 and D7 look empty, but actually they contain space!

In this way, cells will contain either relevant values, or the space character, and will never be empty. Therefore, the problem we were facing earlier will not occur.

Exercise: Entering Data in a Designed Form

1. Open the file **designed form.**
2. Enter the data in the blue marked cells.
3. Create a button to run the macro that will transfer the data to the worksheet **Accumulated data.**
4. Add a border to the table in **Accumulated data** sheet (remember to use shortcut keys to select the table).
5. Return to the designed form and clear the form (delete the data that was entered).
6. Hide the **Accumulated data** worksheet.
7. Place the cursor in the student name field.

Dividing Up the Task

1. Preparations:

   a. Hide the worksheet **Accumulated data**, so you can record the macro without revealing it.

   b. Create helper cells that will contain the data with the IF functions.

2. Make sure that '**Use Relative Reference**' is not active.

3. Select the data.

4. Copy it.

5. Unhide the **Accumulated data** worksheet. Please note you will be taken to this sheet by default, but the sheet doesn't get activated here.

6. Click on the "Form" sheet and click back on the "Accumulative data" worksheet. These two steps activate our "Accumulative data" worksheet.

7. Select the **Accumulated data** worksheet.

8. Select Cell A1, this activates the sheet.

9. Move to a A1000 (distant location).

10. Press the shortcut **Ctrl+Up key.**

11. Switch to Relative Reference.

12. Move down one cell.

13. Paste the data as values that you previously copied.

14. Hide the data collecting worksheet.

15. Press **Esc** to exit selection.

16. Switch back to Absolute Reference.

17. Clear the form.

18. Place the cursor in cell B3.

19. Stop recording.

Excel Tip: Minimizing the Work Area

*Although it is impossible to delete rows or columns in Excel and reduce the worksheet size, we can hide unused rows and columns. We will select the first row of the range we would like to hide, and press the shortcut **Ctrl+Shift+Down key.***

Now, after all the rows have been selected, we will right-click → **'Hide'.**

*We will then repeat these actions with the columns. We will select the first column of the range we would like to hide and press the shortcut **Ctrl+Shift+Right key.***

Now, after all the columns have been selected, we will press right-click → **'Hide'.**

And now we have a form in the desired size.

Excel tip: Worksheet Protection

We often create Excel files which we don't want to be editable. We may either want to prevent modifications to the entire worksheet or only to some selected cells.

The way to do it is by using the option **'Protect Sheet'.**

Protecting the Entire Worksheet

On the **'Review'** *tab select* **'Protect Sheet':**

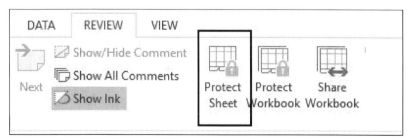

A window will appear where you will be asked to select the desired protections:

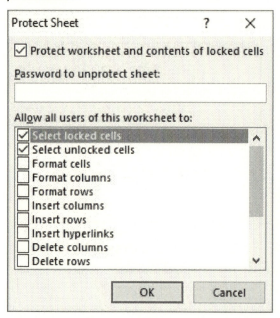

*You will be able to password protect the worksheet. To complete the operation press '**OK**'.*

Now, every attempt to change the date will prompt the following message:

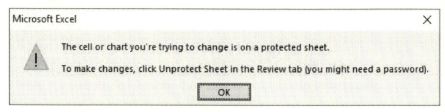

Removing the Worksheet Protection:

*Press '**Unprotect Sheet**'*

If you have password protected your worksheet, you'll be asked to enter it:

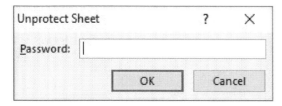

Protecting Part of the Worksheet

*Selecting '**Protect Sheet**' protects the entire worksheet; however, sometimes we want to protect only specific cells or ranges, allowing free access to all others.*

This process is comprised of two steps:

    a. Selecting which cells we want to protect and which we don't.

    b. The protection itself.

Selecting which cells we want to protect and which we don't

*The selection is done on the '**Protection**' tab in the '**Format cells**' window.*

*We will right-click on any cell → '**Format Cells**'*

*'**Format Cells**' window will appear, and we'll select the tab '**Protection**':*

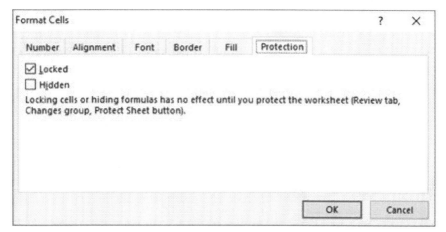

Note, that the cell is '**Locked**' by default.

This means that when selecting '**Protect Sheet**' the cell will be locked.

Since by default the cell's lock is checked, which means active, pressing '**Protect Sheet**' locks all the cells and prevents editing.

It is important to note that as long as the worksheet hasn't been protected the check has no effect.

Unchecking the 'Locked' means that when pressing '**Protect Sheet**', the cell will not be locked.

Removing the lock is not limited only to single cell, but we can do this over a range as well!

And if we want to enable writing in the entire worksheet except for few cells?

In this case we will select the entire worksheet, by pressing the grey triangle between the row numbers and the column letters:

Now we will right-click, choose '**Format Cells**', and on '**Protection**' tab uncheck '**Locked**' and approve.

All the worksheet cells are now marked as unlocked.

Now, we will mark the cells that we do want to protect, right-click and check '**Locked**'.

Pressing '**Protect Sheet**' will lock only the selected cells.

Standard Table

Over the many years I've been working with Excel, I occasionally come across databases that are supposed to be standard, but are actually presented as a report.

One of the common examples is the following table:

Sales	Region
North	196
	184
	129
	194
South	110
	136
	132
	107
Center	190
	116
	125
	184
	198

This table is problematic for two reasons:

a. It has merged cells that prevent performing many Excel operations.

b. The result of canceling the merge is empty cells, which means that some of the sales have no region attached to it, as demonstrated in the next figure:

Sales	Region
North	196
	184
	129
	194

There are many ways to fix the data, such as dragging the regions to fill in the missing data, using formulas, and more.

In this chapter we will demonstrate the quickest and cleverest way to fix the table, but first, we have to learn a few topics:

Excel Tip: Filling a Range of Cells with the Same Value

In the example below we have selected the range B3:E8:

◢	A	B	C	D	E
1					
2					
3					
4					
5					
6					
7					
8					
9					
10					

The active cell in this range is B3.

*Please pay attention to the status '**Ready**' at the bottom of the screen:*

It means that the cell is ready for data entering.

*What happens when we start typing in the active cell? Note that the status changes to '**Enter**':*

108

After we finish typing, and the status is still 'Enter', if we press
Ctrl+Enter *all the range will be filled with the same value!*

If you accidently pressed Enter, the range will not be filled with
the active cell's value and you will have to repeat the action

---

Excel Tip: Selecting Empty Cells

In the next table we would like to select all the empty cells.

For this purpose, we will select the entire column A by pressing its
name in the header, and select on the **'Home'** *tab → '***Find & Select***'*
*→ '***Go To Special***':*

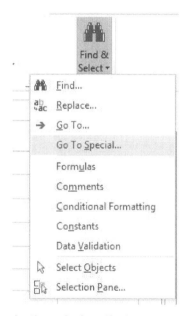

*In the window that appears, we will check '***Blanks***' and press 'OK'*

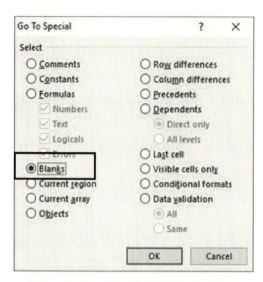

Notice that out of the entire range only the empty cells have been selected:

Sales	Region
North	196
	184
	129
	194
South	110
	136
	132
	107
Center	190
	116
	125
	184
	198

Excel Tip: Paste as Values

Sometimes after performing calculations, we want to turn them into values, i.e. remove the formula and keep only the value of the final result in the cell. The incentive may be hiding the calculation or a big file which is too heavy and we want to reduce its size. The way to do that is to copy the desired range, right-click the

location where we want to paste, and select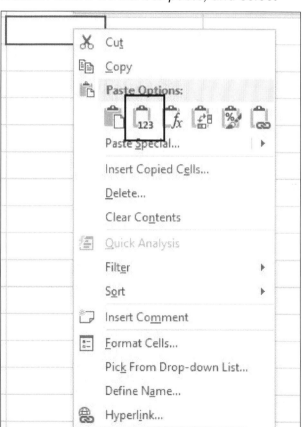

In older versions you'll have to select '**Paste Special**' and in the window that will appear check '**Values**':

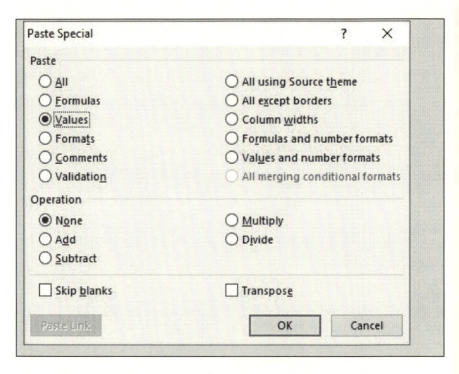

Now, let's combine these three tips to quickly fill in the table:

Exercise: Fixing the Data in a Table

1. Open the file **standard table** in the worksheet **January.**

2. Record a macro named **FixTable.**

3. Select column A (make sure Absolute Reference is used).

4. On '**Home**' tab, '**Alignment**' group, press the arrow next to '**Merge & Center**' to open the drop down menu, and select '**Unmerge Cells**'

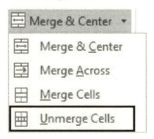

(Be careful not to use '**Merge & Center**' to remove the merge, use only '**Unmerge Cells**'.)

5. Select '**Find & Select**' → '**Go To Special**' → '**Blanks**'.
6. The active cell is A3.
7. Type in it the formula =A2.
8. To finish press **Ctrl+Enter**.
9. The empty cells have just received the right values.
10. Select column A.
11. Copy it.
12. Select cell A1.
13. Paste as values.
14. Press **Esc** to remove the dotted line.
15. Select cell A1.
16. Stop recording.
17. Run the macro on **February** worksheet.
18. Run the macro on **March** worksheet.

Pivot Table

We often receive monthly or quarterly data, mostly from other systems' output, sometimes from other departments.

In order to efficiently analyze the data and compare the values of different time periods, or different departments, we have to collect the data from the separate tables to one central table.

The following table is a collection of all support calls, and as you can see, currently it contains the data of January-March. Later on, next months' support calls will be added:

	A	B	C	D
1	Call ID	Date	Call Reason	Representative
2	A1000	01/01/15	technical	Michael
3	A1001	01/01/15	technical	Michael
4	A1002	01/01/15	technical	David
5	A1003	01/01/15	new client	Lisa
6	A1004	01/02/15	financial	Brett
7	A1005	01/02/15	disconnect	David
8	A1006	01/02/15	financial	Rick
9	A1007	01/02/15	new client	Rick
10	A1008	01/02/15	new client	Roi
11	A1009	01/02/15	technical	Brett
12	A1010	01/03/15	financial	Brett
13	A1011	01/03/15	financial	May
14	A1012	01/03/15	financial	Rick
15	A1013	01/03/15	financial	naomi
16	A1014	01/03/15	financial	Roi
17	A1015	01/03/15	new client	May
18	A1016	01/03/15	technical	Brett
19	A1017	01/03/15	new client	Lisa
20	A1018	01/03/15	financial	Rick
21	A1019	01/04/15	new client	David
22	A1020	01/04/15	disconnect	Roi
23	A1021	01/04/15	disconnect	Rick
24	A1022	01/04/15	disconnect	Lisa

Out of this table we have created a pivot table, which presents the monthly call number and additionally compares month to month. (In February for example, we had 144 calls which is 6 less calls than January's support calls number.)

Date ▾	Calls	Compare to Prev Month
Jan	150	
Feb	144	-6
Mar	31	-113
Grand Total	325	

The monthly value comparison is one of the pivot table's built-in options[1]. Now we have to build a macro to collect the new data added each quarter, add it to the existing data, and finally refresh the pivot table to present a month to month comparison.

In the following example we will have a simple pivot table that presents the number of support calls per representative in each time period.

Since we would like the pivot table to present the existing data in the table, which as mentioned changes its size every quarter, we have to instruct Excel to update the range on which the pivot table is based, according to the actual record number.

In order to avoid changing the range manually, the pivot table will be based on a dynamic table (see page 71), so any changes in the table will be reflected in the pivot table after refreshing.

Before we start, let's observe the sequence of steps:

1. Turning the table on which the pivot table is based to a dynamic table.

---

[1] To read more about the smart analysis that can be performed using pivot tables, refer to the book *Pivot Tables - Smart Data Analysis* by Maayan Poleg at http://amzn.to/1N1x1Hm (case sensitive)

2. Creating a pivot table layout.

3. Copying the periodic table data.

4. Pasting the data at the end of the collecting table.

5. Refreshing the pivot table.

I remind you that since we have to paste the quarterly data at the end of the previous quarterly data, we have to navigate to the first empty cell at the edge of the table. We can place the cursor in a distant cell and move it up using the shortcut **Ctrl+Up key,** and then move one cell down using Relative Reference.

So what is the problem? Creating the main file!

First, we have to type the header then turn the table to a dynamic one to allow its range to increase automatically each time we paste the quarterly data:

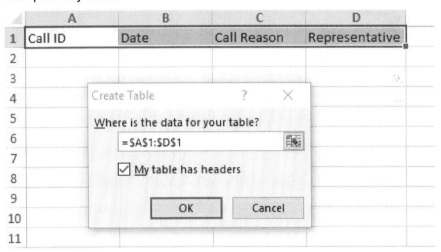

After creating the dynamic table, we will have this one:

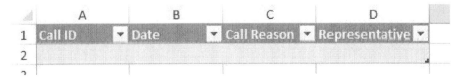

Notice that this is an empty table, but its first row, although it does not contain data, is included in the table's range.

When we move up from a distant cell below, we will navigate to cell A2 and paste the data there.

But what would happen after pasting one quarter's data?

	A	B	C	D
1	Call ID ▾	Date ▾	Call Reason ▾	Representative ▾
2	A1000	01/01/15	technical	Michael
3	A1001	01/01/15	technical	Michael
4	A1002	01/01/15	technical	David
5	A1003	01/01/15	new client	Lisa
6	A1004	01/02/15	financial	Brett
7	A1005	01/02/15	disconnect	David
8				

Notice that this time the last cell in the table is not empty, and therefore after navigating to it, we will have to move one cell down using Relative Reference.

That is, the first time we run the macro, we need to stay in the cell to which we navigate using **Ctrl+Up key**, but in all the following runs, we will have to move one cell down.

This means, the action that is taken when adding the first file is different than those we have to take when adding the next files!

So what is the solution?

We will manually create the pivot table that will be based on the first quarter data, and record the macro only when the second file will be added to the main file.

That is, if there is a difference between the first macro run and all the rest of the runs, we will record the macro starting on the second run.

118

For the next exercise, open the file **Pivot Table - Full** and take a look at the two worksheets. In the **data** worksheet you'll find the first quarter data, and in the **analysis** worksheet you'll find the pivot table.

Close the file.

Exercise: Pivot Table

1. Open the file **Pivot Table - 2nd Qtr.**
2. Record a macro named **AddDataToMain**.
3. Save it in '**Personal Macro Workbook**', so it will be available to all files.
4. Using Absolute Reference select cell A2.
5. Select the table. Notice that since you have to copy the table without the headers, you won't be able to use the shortcut **Ctrl+*** , and you'll have to select cell A2. Use **Ctrl+Shift+Right Key** to select the entire row 2, and then **Ctrl+Shift+Down key** to select all other rows.
6. Copy the data.
7. On the '**File**' tab → '**Open**' open the file '**Pivot Table – Full**'.
8. Select the worksheet **data** (even if it is already the active worksheet).
9. Verify that '**Use Relative Reference**' is not active.
10. Place the cursor in a distant cell, for example A10000 (a cell that will surely be empty).
11. Use the shortcut **Ctrl+Up key** to navigate to the last non-empty cell.
12. Switch to Relative Reference.
13. Move the cursor one cell down.

119

14. Paste.

15. Switch to worksheet **Analysis.**

16. Select the first cell of the pivot table and refresh it.

17. Use the shortcut **Ctrl+S** to save the file.

18. Stop recording.

Now you can close both files and repeat the exercise with the new data in the file **Pivot Table - 3rd Qtr**.

Printing

One of the most common operations is printing. We can record a macro that will contain all the print settings: adding a logo to a header, page numbering, changing the page orientation to landscape, fitting to page, and more.

Excel Tip: Fit the Worksheet to Paper

Our data ranges do not depend on the physical page size and can be wider or longer. If we want to fit the data range to one page only, we can do it in the following way:

*On the '**Page Layout**' tab, click the arrow in the right bottom of the '**Page Setup**' group:*

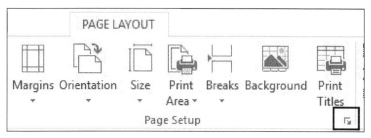

*'**Page Setup**' window will appear:*

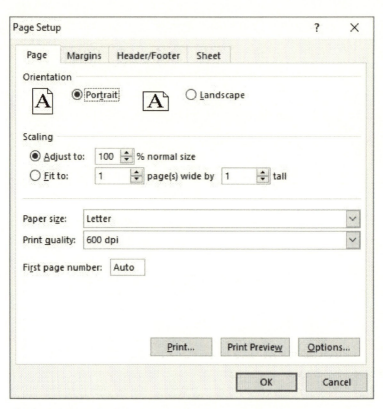

If the data slightly exceeds the page size, we can scale the worksheet percentage, for example – 80% of normal size:

If we desire to force the data into one page, and we want Excel to compute the percentage, we need to select the option 'Fit to':

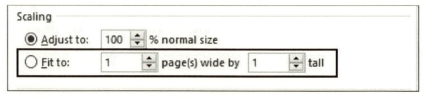

And if we want to shrink the data to fit all columns in the same page without limiting the number of pages because we can't predict the row's number, we will leave the box 'tall' empty:

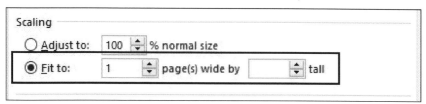

Excel Tip: Repeating Column Headings

When we print tables that spread over a few pages, we would like the headings to appear on top of each page.

On the tab 'Page Layout' in group 'Sheet Options' press the arrow on the right bottom:

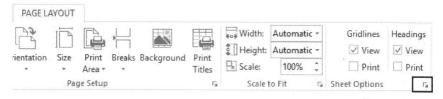

The following window will appear:

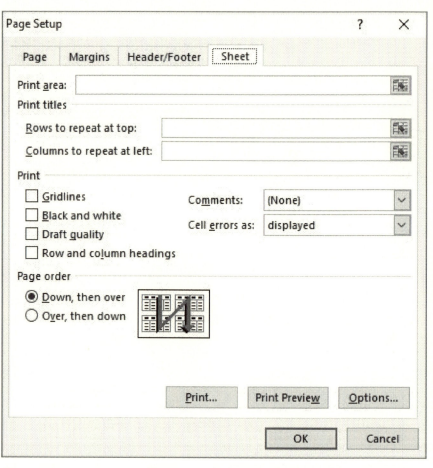

Place the cursor on '**Rows to repeat at top**' and select the headings row in the worksheet:

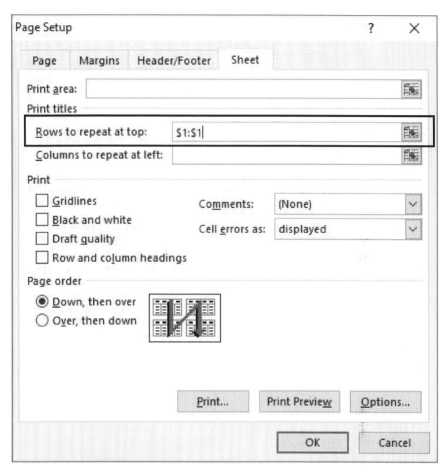

Now the heading will appear in each one of the printed pages.

Excel Tip: Adding a Logo

In order to make our printed pages look professional, it is customary to add the company's logo.

*Go to '**Page Settings**' as we have learned in the previous tips, and select the tab '**Header/Footer**':*

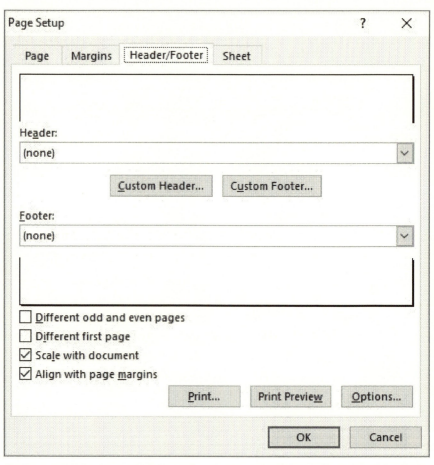

Since we want to add the logo to the Header, we need to select
'Custom Header...'

The following window will appear:

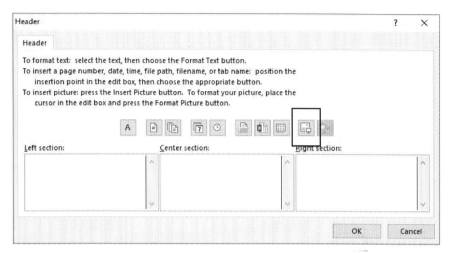

The Header is divided into three sections. Select the part where you want to add the logo. In my case I'm selecting the left section, and press '**Insert Picture**'.

Now navigate to the desired picture and press '**Insert**', and '**OK**' to complete the action.

When printing the worksheet, the logo will be printed on each page.

Excel Tip: Adding Page Numbers

The tab "**Header/Footer**' that was presented in the previous tip enables also to add page numbers to the printed pages.

Select the location of the footer (right, center, left section), and press [icon]. The numbers will be added.

Importing a Text File

Excel has a built-in wizard which enables importing data in txt format file. The wizard has a few steps which enable selecting the file format, the starting row for import, the columns to import and which not, the column data format, and more.

Excel Tip: Importing a Text File

1. On *'Data'* tab, *'Get External Data'* group select *'From Text'*

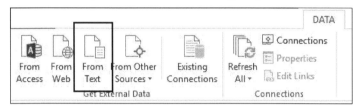

2. In the window that will appear, navigate to the text file *MyData.txt.*

3. The Text Import Wizard will be launched:

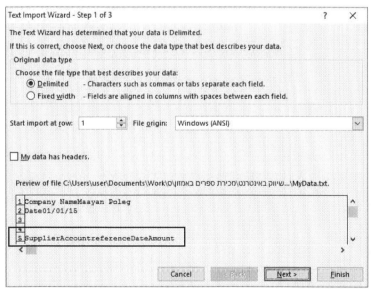

4. Select the import start row, in our case 5.

5. Press Next >.

6. Select the delimiter:

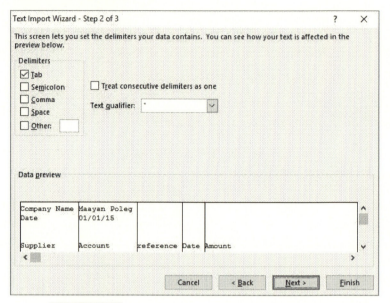

7. Press Next >.

8. *In the third step, you are able to select each column and set the data format, choose whether it should be imported or not, and in case of a date you can select the date format (MDY/ DMY etc).*

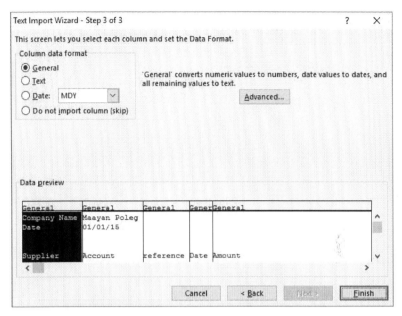

9. Press *'Finish'*.

10. A window *will appear and you'll be asked where you want to put the data.*

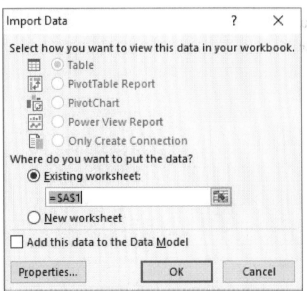

11. *To complete* the *action press 'OK'.*

12. The file content will now appear in Excel!

Comment: The import as presented above works properly, but in some cases you may get the following error message

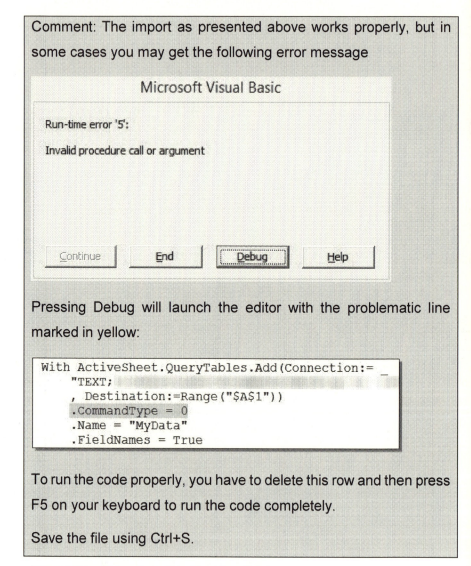

Pressing Debug will launch the editor with the problematic line marked in yellow:

```
With ActiveSheet.QueryTables.Add(Connection:= _
    "TEXT;
    , Destination:=Range("$A$1"))
    .CommandType = 0
    .Name = "MyData"
    .FieldNames = True
```

To run the code properly, you have to delete this row and then press F5 on your keyboard to run the code completely.

Save the file using Ctrl+S.

Excel Tip: Freezing the Header Row

In the chapter where we discussed printing, we've learned how to repeat the header in each printed page; however, since we work mostly on screen and when we scroll down the screen the header

*disappears, we will learn how to display the header in a long data range. This is done using '**Freeze Panes**' on the '**View**' tab.*

1. *Place the cursor in the data range.*

2. *Press '**Freeze Panes**'.*

3. *The following options will appear:*

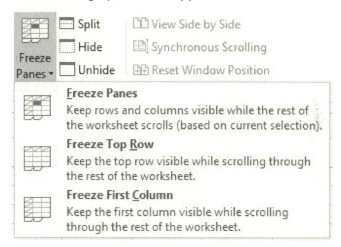

4. *If the data includes a header select '**Freeze Top Row**'.*

5. *If you want to freeze the first row (which usually contains identifer such as Id. number, license plate number, or catalog number) select '**Freeze First Column**'.*

We often want to freeze both the first row and the first column, or few rows and few columns.

*In order to do that, we have to place the cursor in the cell below and right to the rows and columns that we want to freeze, and then select '**Freeze Panes**'.*

The following examples will clarify where to place the cursor:

If we want to freeze the first two top rows and the left column, we will place the cursor in cell B3 because it has two rows above it and one column to the left. To illustrate that, I marked the cells that we want to freeze gray:

133

And if we want to freeze the three top rows and the first two columns, we will place the cursor in cell C4, because it has three rows on top it and two columns on the left:

Exercise: Importing a Text File

1. Record a macro to import the text file **MyData.txt** to an Excel file.

2. While importing, format the date column by selecting a date format.

3. After importing:

   a.   Format the total column by selecting the thousands separator.

b.   Adjust the column widths.

c.   Freeze the header row.

4. Where should you save the recorded macro to be able to run it each time on a new text file?

Testing the Recorded Macro

After recording a macro and before using it, we should perform tests to verify that it works properly.

In this chapter I have collected the most important tests:

Cursor's Position

Since we do not know the cursor's position before running the macro, we need to proactively move it to the location where we want it to be when we start recording.

For example, if our data range always starts in cell A1, we'll record the shortcut Ctrl+Home, before we begin the series of actions.

We will do this even if the cursor is already in cell A1!

Navigation Direction

In some cases it is better to start at the end of the data and work backwards. For example: In case we need to get to the last cell, and we have no way of knowing how many empty cells exist in the data, we will navigate to the last cell and progress upwards from there.

Cursor's Location is Inside/Outside the Range

Run the macro with the cursor placed inside the range and when it is outside of it.

Test on a Larger/Smaller Table than the Original Table

Does the macro work on tables different in size than the one you used for the recording?

Outside 'close' / Outside 'far'

Place the cursor a short distance outside the table and run the macro.

Rerun the macro when the cursor is located outside the table, far away from it. That is, if the table has 4 columns, place the cursor in a distance <u>larger</u> than 4 columns away, and the same applies to the number of rows.

When the Table is Full/Has Only One Line

Check what happens when the macro runs on a table filled with data and when it contains only the header row.

What happens when there is no data at all?

Missing Data

Does your macro work both when the data in the table is complete and when data is missing?

What happens if the data is missing from the first row?

It is important to perform this test mainly on key fields. These are the table's identifier fields, such as an ID number, license plate number and so on.

First Macro Run/All Other Macro Runs

- There might be situations where running the macro for the first time will require a different approach than the next runs. In these cases record the macro only after you've already run it manually the first time.

Limitations of the Recording and the Recorded Macro

Despite the many possibilities in macro recording, there are some limitations that should be considered. Most of them can be solved by writing a VBA code.

In macro recording it is impossible to:

- loop through a data range
- define variables
- call a macro from within another macro
- combine two macros
- edit a macro while recording it
- modify a macro after the recording ended
- use UNDO (after the macro ran it is impossible to undo the actions)
- create graphs based on dynamic ranges
- If your macro creates objects with names (for example – to a pivot table, Excel gives automatically the name PivotTable1, the following table PivotTable2 and the same applies for graphs and dynamic tables), you may run into a problem if you run the macro on the same file again and again because the macro you recorded will refer to PivotTable1 while the new pivot table you have created has the name PivotTable2.

FAQ

This chapter was written as a result of various questions raised by students in my courses.

My tables are identical in their structure, but located in different positions on the worksheet. How can I record a macro that will always navigate to the table's top?

Great question!

First of all, tables are not supposed to be located in different positions. A standard table will always start in cell A1, and will not have any empty rows or empty columns.

And now, after the tirade, here's the solution:

Since this is actually the same table which only changes location, you can use Excel's search option and locate the first occurrence of a word that appears at the beginning of the table.

Assuming it is the title 'product', follow the guidelines below:

1. Open the file **Format a table with Unknown Location.**
2. Switch to worksheet 1.
3. Record a macro named **SelectTbl.**
4. Press the shortcut **Ctrl+Home.**
5. Click the '**Editing**' → '**Find and Replace**' (or the shortcut **Ctrl+F**).
6. Type in the '**Find what**' box the word 'product'.
7. Use the shortcut **Ctrl+*** to mark the entire table.
8. Add borders.
9. Stop recording.

10. Run the code you recorded on the table in worksheet 2.

If the table begins at A1 you will get an error message when you try to move up one cell.

If you see that your table is standard, don't run the code.

How do I select the entire table, except for the header rows?

As we have learned, selecting an entire table is done using the shortcut **Ctrl+*** (if the data range should change its size) or **Ctrl+A** (if the range is constant).

But what would we do if we wish to select the table without the header row?

In this case, we will select cell A2, press **Ctrl+Shift+Right Key** to select the first row and then **Ctrl+Shift** +Down key to select the other rows.

We can also use the shortcut **Ctrl+Shift+End** when the cursor is placed in cell A2.

Note that both options could be problematic.

In the first option, if one of the cells in the first row is empty, pressing Shift+Right key column will reach the last column, so the entire table will not be selected.

The shortcuts Ctrl+* or Ctrl+A may also be problematic, because if there is additional data beyond the table's edge it will be selected together with the table that we want to copy.

In addition, there are cases where it seems there is no data outside the table, but Excel still selects a bigger range. This problem can occur when previously there was data in a remote cell that although has been deleted, Excel still considers it the 'end of the data'. This situation often occurs when receiving data from an external system and Excel considers the worksheet edge the end of the data.

Therefore, you have to know your table's structure and choose the most appropriate method accordingly.

How do I record a macro for formatting a cell and automatically adjusting column width?

When we recorded our first macro (page 34) we formatted it using different tabs or shortcuts.

However, what would happen if we would also want to extend the column automatically, so whenever we select a range and run the macro on it the columns will change their width to fit the text?

Our natural tendency is to double-click the line that separates the columns to expand the cell.

So why shouldn't we do it?

All the actions in the exercise were performed on the selected range, without moving the cursor. However, double-click moves the cursor out of the selected cell and makes another selection, which **is recorded into the code**.

Therefore, if we want to format cells or ranges, we will try to use as much as possible the commands that are on the various tabs instead of making mouse selections.

By the way, adjusting the cell's width to the text size is on the 'Home' tab → group 'Cells' → 'Format' → 'AutoFit Column Width'.

Remove Duplicates

Remove Duplicates is one of the refreshing innovations of the ribbon versions. (In Excel 2003 it was well hidden under the Advanced Filter option and was less convenient to use) But while trying to use this option on variable-size tables, we will realize that it is based on a fixed size table. Even if we record a macro that selects an entire column, and we ask to remove duplicates, Excel will record the table size as it was when recording, so when the macro runs on larger tables, not all duplicates will be removed.

Before we learn how to remove duplicates using a macro, I want to show you how Excel enables removing duplicates, because this is an important and effective option to know!

Let's look at the following list:

	A
1	representative
2	Dan
3	David
4	Rachel
5	Rachel
6	Rachel
7	Rachel
8	David
9	Dan
10	Dan
11	Dan
12	David
13	Rachel
14	David
15	Rachel
16	Rachel
17	Dan
18	Dan
19	Dan

The objective is to create a list of representatives, each appearing only once.

1. Place the cursor in any cell in the list. (It is preferable to place it in the header row since it certainly contains data.)

2. Switch to '**Data**' tab.

3. Press

4. The following window will appear:

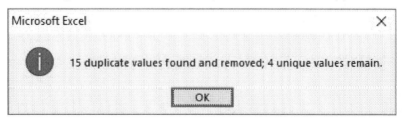

5. If your data has headers check the box.

6. Press 'OK'.

7. A message on the number of duplicates found will appear:

8. Press 'OK'.

9. A new list will be created which includes each value only once:

	A
1	representative
2	Dan
3	David
4	Rachel

If the data range contains more than one column, we can choose which combination of data is considered unique. You might want to produce a list of representatives' names or a unique list of names and support reasons, with the representative name appearing once per each reason.

But, as we have mentioned before, removing duplicates operates on a fixed size range. So how is it possible to record a macro and remove duplicates to create unique records? This will be demonstrated in the following tips:

Excel Tip: Counting the Occurrences of a Certain Value

We often want to know the number of occurrences of a specific value in the table.

*The way to do this is using the function **CountIf**, that counts values that meet certain criteria, and this is its syntax:*

=COUNTIF(Range, Criteria)

The following example will illustrate the use of the function:

Our table has a list of support calls to our service center, and we want to know the number of occurrences of each representative:

146

	A
1	Representative
2	Michael
3	Michael
4	David
5	Lisa
6	Lisa
7	Rick
8	naomi
9	Roi
10	Michael
11	Michael
12	Rick
13	Michael
14	Michael
15	David

If we want to know how often Michael appears, we will write the following function:

=COUNTIF(A2:A15,A2)

That is, our range is A2:A15 and the criterion is the value that appears in cell A2, in our case, Dan.

In words, "How many times does Dan appear in the range A2:A15? "

And if we want to drag the formula across all rows, then of course we need to convert the reference to the range to absolute, as can be seen in the following example:

	A	B	C
1	Representative	Formula	Count
2	Michael	=COUNTIF($A$2:$A$15,A2)	4
3	Michael	=COUNTIF($A$2:$A$15,A3)	4
4	David	=COUNTIF($A$2:$A$15,A4)	2
5	Lisa	=COUNTIF($A$2:$A$15,A5)	2
6	Lisa	=COUNTIF($A$2:$A$15,A6)	2
7	Rick	=COUNTIF($A$2:$A$15,A7)	2
8	naomi	=COUNTIF($A$2:$A$15,A8)	1
9	Roi	=COUNTIF($A$2:$A$15,A9)	1
10	Michael	=COUNTIF($A$2:$A$15,A10)	4
11	Michael	=COUNTIF($A$2:$A$15,A11)	4
12	Rick	=COUNTIF($A$2:$A$15,A12)	2
13	May	=COUNTIF($A$2:$A$15,A13)	1
14	Brett	=COUNTIF($A$2:$A$15,A14)	1
15	David	=COUNTIF($A$2:$A$15,A15)	2
16			

Now, let's examine another issue: I would like to display 1 for the first value occurance, 2 for the second, and so on. This is demonstrated in the following tip:

Running Count of Value Occurrence in List

To continue the previous tip's example, I would like to display the count for each instance, so the first time Michael appears will get the number 1, the second time will get the number 2 and so on.

The way to do this is by making the beginning Cell Address of the range to absolute, but not its end!

In this way, when we drag the formula, the range will increase in each row.

The initial formula is:

=COUNTIF($A$2:A2,A2)

That is, we are looking for Michael (found in cell A2), in a range which size is currently one cell, A2.

148

But what happens when we drag the formula?

Since the beginning of the range is absolute, the beginning of the range always remains at A2, however, since we didn't convert to absolute the end of the range, A2 will change to A3, A3 to A4 and so on, as you can see in the following example:

	A	B	C
1	Representative	Formula	Count
2	Michael	=COUNTIF($A$2:A2,A2)	1
3	Michael	=COUNTIF($A$2:A3,A3)	2
4	David	=COUNTIF($A$2:A4,A4)	1
5	Lisa	=COUNTIF($A$2:A5,A5)	1
6	Lisa	=COUNTIF($A$2:A6,A6)	2
7	Rick	=COUNTIF($A$2:A7,A7)	1
8	naomi	=COUNTIF($A$2:A8,A8)	1
9	Roi	=COUNTIF($A$2:A9,A9)	1
10	Michael	=COUNTIF($A$2:A10,A10)	3
11	Michael	=COUNTIF($A$2:A11,A11)	4
12	Rick	=COUNTIF($A$2:A12,A12)	2
13	May	=COUNTIF($A$2:A13,A13)	1
14	Brett	=COUNTIF($A$2:A14,A14)	1
15	David	=COUNTIF($A$2:A15,A15)	2
16			

If you check the number of occurrences you will see that Michael in the first row received the number 1, because we have limited the range only to the first time it appears.

In row 2 he received the value 2, because we have expanded the range and this is indeed its second occurrence, and in row 10 he received the number 3, because it is the third occurrence in the extended range.

Excel Tip: Creating Unique Records Without Using 'Remove Duplicates'

If you have a list in which there are repeated values, and you want to generate a list where each value appears only once, you can use the previous tip as a basis.

We will add a formula that counts the occurrences of each representative and assigns them running numbers, then we will delete all rows with values bigger than 1.

Exercise: Creating Unique Records

1. Open the file '**Unique Records**'.
2. Record a new macro named **Unique_Rec.**
3. Using Absolute Reference, select cell B1 and enter the header '**Count**'.
4. Select cell B2 and type in it the following formula:

=COUNTIF($A$2:A2,A2)

5. Finish typing the formula by using the shortcut **Ctrl+Enter.**
6. Drag the formula to a distant cell (one that you are sure will never contain data).
7. Press the shortcut **Ctrl+Down key.** (Now the cursor is in the last cell that contains a formula.)
8. Using Relative reference, select one cell to the left.
9. Press the shortcut **Ctrl+Up key**.
10. Make sure that you are using Relative Reference and move the cursor one cell down.
11. Now you are in the first cell that has no representative name.
12. Move the cursor one cell right to select the first cell where the formula is not relevant.

150

13. Select the shortcut **Ctrl+Shift+**Down key to select all the redundant formulas.

14. Press delete on your keyboard.

15. Press the shortcut **Ctrl+Home** to place the cursor at the top of the table.

16. Switch to '**Data**' tab and press Filter .

17. In the Filter arrow, select the value 1. A list of all representatives that appear the first time will be displayed

18. Select the entire table by using the shortcut **Ctrl+***.

19. Copy it.

20. Add a new worksheet using the ⊕ (in 2013) or (in 2010) and paste the new table.

21. Delete the counting formulas column.

22. Stop recording.

And for Those Interested – Nevertheless VBA...

If you read up to this point, I'm sure you enriched yourself and improved your Excel skills. In this chapter I would like to give you a small glimpse of the recorded code and teach you a few tricks to help you overcome some of the limitations of the recorded macros.

I remind you again, backup your files before changing them in any way.

Viewing a Macro

Select on '**Developer**' tab →

In the window that appears, select the desired macro and press '**Edit**':

This will launch the VBA editor, and you will be able to view the recorded macro:

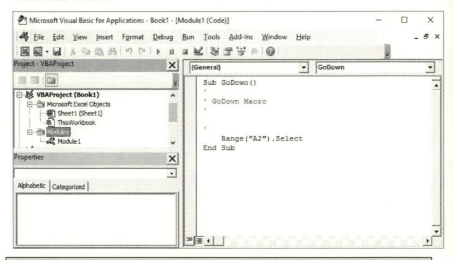

Reading the code, you will be able to understand a large part of it even if you are still not able to write it yourself!

Combining Macro Commands

Sometimes we have to record a long macro, and we prefer recording it in parts. The problem in this case is that each part is recorded as a separate macro and to run the complete macro, we have to run each one of the macro parts separately. However, a simple edit using a VBA Editor will easily call one macro from the other, and thus run all the macros at once, rather than each of them separately.

How do we do it?

First, we have to know where the macro name is.

If we look at the code that we recorded earlier, we can find the name immediately after the word Sub and in our case, the macro name is **Select_A2**.

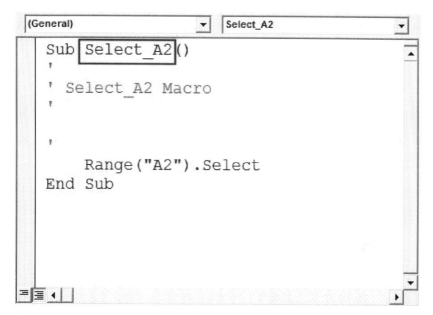

Now, let's take a look at the other macro code, which changes the selected column's width to 20:

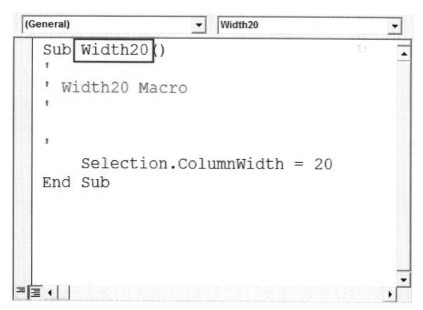

And if I wish to combine the two commands?

All I have to do is to copy the macro name from the first code, and paste it at the end of the second code.

In our case, after changing the column width to 20, I would like to select the cell A2, and so I will paste the code name Select_A2 at the end of the first code (before the End Sub):

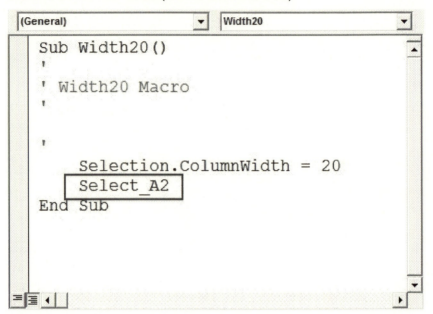

You can also copy the entire macro content and paste it at the end of the first macro (without the Sub and End Sub lines), but I find that copying the name line to be easier.

Combining Exercise

1. Open the file **combine.**
2. Record a macro named **RedFont** that formats the data in red font, size 14
3. Stop recording.
4. Record another macro named **MyBorder** that adds border to the table.

5. Stop recording.

6. Combine the two macros.

7. Run the combined macro.

Cleaning the Code

If you use a macro recording as a preliminary step to write code in VBA, I recommend that you edit the recorded code and examine it. You will quickly learn that macro recording, as opposed to manual coding, is wasteful and records extra actions and features.

When you view the code, you can safely delete the following commands:

- Comments
- Mouse scrolling
- The structure WITH

as explained in the following sections:

Comments

Each line begins with an apostrophe (') and painted in green, is a comment line. At the top of each code several lines of comments appear, some empty and some with content. If, for example, you add some description of the macro or define shortcut keys, the information will appear in comment lines, as you can see in the following screenshot:

```
Sub Select_A2()
'
' Select_A2 Macro
' Macro for selectin A2

'

    Range("A2").Select
End Sub
```

To save space, you may delete the comment lines.

On the other hand, you can add comments to the code by typing an apostrophe followed by the comment.

Scrolling

Sometimes our macro recording includes scrolling the screen to reach the desired cell.

Since scrolling does not contribute to the code, you can delete it.

Below is a screenshot of the code generated when scrolling the screen using scroll bars, and selecting cell A100:

```
Sub SelectA100()
    ActiveWindow.SmallScroll Down:=90
    Range("A100").Select
End Sub
```

You can safely delete every line starting with:

158

ActiveWindow.SmallScroll

ActiveWindow.ScrollColumn

ActiveWindow.ScrollRow

WITH Structure

We wish to record a code to center the data in a cell.

Recording generates the following code:

```
Sub MyCenter()

    With Selection
        .HorizontalAlignment = xlCenter
        .VerticalAlignment = xlBottom
        .WrapText = False
        .Orientation = 0
        .AddIndent = False
        .IndentLevel = 0
        .ShrinkToFit = False
        .ReadingOrder = xlContext
        .MergeCells = False
    End With

End Sub
```

A series of commands apear between the structure statements **With Selection** and **End With**, and although we changed only one feature (horizontal alignment), the generated code contains many features. The sharp-eyed among you will notice that this is actually a copy of the '**Alignment**' tab in the '**Format Cells**' window:

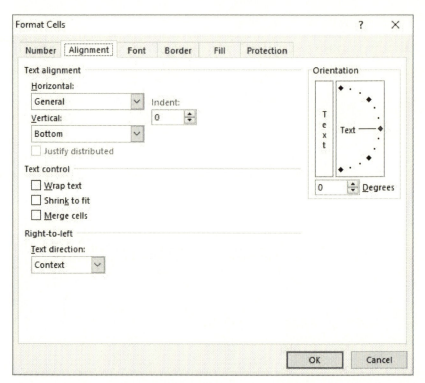

In fact, the macro editor recorded all options available in this window, although we didn't perform any changes in them.

Although the commands are written in VBA, a basic level of English is sufficient to find the one line relevant to our code:

```
.HorizontalAlignment = xlCenter
```

The rest of the lines are redundant, slow down the running code, and make it difficult to read. Therefore, we will delete all the lines that we don't need, as long as we are careful to keep the commands in the following structure:

```
With Selection

      . Command

End With
```

And in our case:

```
Sub MyCenter()

    With Selection
        .VerticalAlignment = xlCenter
    End With

End Sub
```

Before you delete a row, you can mark it as a comment by adding an apostrophe at the beginning. In this case, if you find out that the line was important for the code, although you had thought that it was not important, you will not have to re-record the macro; just delete the apostrophe that you've added.

Only after you are sure that the code works correctly can you delete all unnecessary lines.

What's Next?

This book has discussed macro recording to create process automation in Excel. If you wish to continue and make progress self-studying, you can do this with the help of the additional books I wrote:

- Excel VBA 2013: For Non-Programmers (Programming in Everyday Language)
- Pivot Tables - Smart Data Analysis

The books can be purchased on Amazon.

Excel VBA For Non Programmers:

http://amzn.to/2cvFvpa (case sensitive)

Excel 2013 Pivot Tables: Smart Data Analysis

http://amzn.to/1N1x1Hm (case sensitive)

Hope to hear from you what benefit you have gained from this book

Maayan Poleg

The book – Excel VBA 2013: For Non-Programmers (Programming in Everyday Language)

 Over the years, Microsoft Excel has become the dominant program in the field of spreadsheets.

However, with the progress and expansion of the use of the software, end users are required to perform tasks that are possible only by programming in VBA.

The book was written as a response to the growing demand for advanced use of all the capabilities of the software.

- Those who want to develop forms, screens and "automats" for the purpose of the organization's information management
- Those who want to make Excel a powerful utility that accompanies the daily work
- The non-programmers among us who have to build the same reports in Excel repeatedly and want to automate these actions

During editing the book I've examined Excel and the VBA editor through the eyes of the end users, who have no background in programming but have a desire to make the most out of the software. Therefore the book was written in plain and simple everyday language, minimizing deliberately the use of technical terms as a result of years of experience in programming and training.

The goal I had set out for myself was to pass the essence of the VBA language and allow those taking their first steps to learn even unaccompanied by a close guide.

<u>And I proudly say that my book is on the bestseller list of Amazon!</u>

 Excel VBA: for Non-Programmers (Programming in Everyday Language) Apr 14, 2014
by Maayan Poleg

Kindle Edition
$7.97
Auto-delivered wirelessly

★★★★☆ ▾ 24

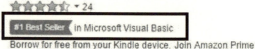 in Microsoft Visual Basic

Paperback
$13.57 *√Prime*
Get it by Monday, Aug 31

Borrow for free from your Kindle device. Join Amazon Prime

Kindle Store: See all 192 items

More Buying Choices
$13.57 used & new (8 offers)

The book Pivot Tables – Smart Data Analysis

- Do your tables contain too much information?

- Can you see patterns and trends at a glance?
- Can you understand the significance of the many figures?
- Can you discover connections in the data by a quick scan?
- Does the data in the tables provide answers about patterns and trends?

Pivot table is a simple, yet powerful technique, allowing the user to convert the data overload into meaningful information for the organization.

Using Pivot Tables enables:

- Viewing the data in dozens of different perspectives with an easy mouse drag
- Performing quick calculations without using formulas
- Focusing on different parts of the data, to get a clear and concise picture
- Presenting more trends and patterns
- Creating dozens of reports and graphs to analyze the data in many views
- Visualizing how different data interacts

The book was written by Maayan Poleg, experienced in Microsoft Excel in general, and in pivot tables in particular.

Pats   Eagles

4   9

2   3

Made in the USA
Columbia, SC
16 January 2018